something delicious

something delicious

100 RECIPES FOR EVERYDAY COOKING

Lindsey Baruch of Lindsey Eats

Photography by Eva Kolenko

TEN SPEED PRESS
California | New York

Contents

What Are We Going to Eat?   9
The Recipe for "Something Delicious"   12
Shop My Kitchen   14
Tools & Tips   17

Snacks & Apps   20

Meyer Lemon & Harissa Wings   22
Ahi Tuna Aguachile Verde with Tostadas   25
Curry & Honey Spiced Nuts   26
Icy Crudités with Roasted Garlic Tarragon Yogurt Dip   28
Caramelized Five-Allium Dip Topped with Salmon Roe   29
Persian Shallot Dip with Sumac & Saffron Chili Crisp   32
Crispy Tempura Cauliflower Tossed in Spicy Miso Mayo   34
Scallop & Radish Crudo with Chile & Citrus   37
Ponzu & Togarashi-Marinated Olives   38

Breads & Spreads   40

Chili Crisp & Strawberry Baked Brie   42
Mushroom "Escargots" with Parsley Butter   45
Danny's Sicilian Pizza with Garlicky Oil   46
Marinated Labneh Balls with Harissa & Aleppo Pepper   52
Panzanella Toast with Sambal Aioli   55
Kashke Bademjan with a Lotta Kashk   56
Shakshuka Rancheros with Zesty Crema   59
Anchovy & Pepperoncini Olive Tapenade Crostini   60
MLT with Very Shallot-y Mayo   63
Rosemary Butter Beans with Heavy Pepper & Pecorino   64

Salad Obsessed   66

Kinda Niçoise with Farro & Smashed Caper Dressing   68
Little Gem Caesar Salad with Habanero Dressing & Sourdough Bread Crumbs   71
Spicy Crushed Cucumber Salad with Feta & Mint   72
Endive & Whole-Grain Mustard Salad   75
Steakhouse Wedge Salad with Gorgonzola Dressing & Bacon Bread Crumbs   76
Beet & Peach Salad with Burrata, Toasted Hazelnuts & Green Goddess Vinaigrette   79
Butter Lettuce & Avocado Salad with Uncle Ira's "Good Dressing"   80
Radicchio & Fennel Salad with Orange Maple Poppy Seed Vinaigrette   83
Cucumber, Cantaloupe & Tomato Salad with Ranch-ish Dressing   84

Cozy Soups, Stews & Broths   86

Turmeric Dal with Minty-Lime Yogurt & Crispy Onions   89
Cream of Broccolini & Smoked Gouda Soup   90
Beet Soup with Fennel, Onions & Horseradish Cream   93
Grandma Daisy's Tomato & Chicken Rice Soup   94
Creamy Tortilla Soup with Chili-Lime Strips   98
White Miso & Scallion Brothy Beans   101
One-Pot French Onion & Shallot Soup with Sourdough Toasts   102
Calabrian Chili Tomato Soup with Pizza-ish Croutons   105
Loaded Baked Potato & Leek Soup with Paprika Butter   106

Pasta & Noodles, Baby!   108

- Buttery Saffron & Sungold Tomato Pasta   111
- Minty Pasta with Hot Italian Sausage & Red Chard   112
- Lamb Bolognese with Fennel & Ricotta   115
- Spicy Peanut Noodles with Snap Peas & Scallions   119
- Hazelnut Pesto Bucatini with Sun-Dried Tomato & Vinegar Bread Crumbs   120
- Soju Gochujang Rigatoni   123
- Mushroom Miso Mascarpone Pappardelle   124
- Caramelized Leek & Cabbage Pasta   127
- Anchovy Harissa Mussels & Linguine   128

Catch of the Day   130

- Ancho Chile Shrimp Tacos with Creamy Avocado Ginger Salsa   133
- Gochujang Slow-Roasted Steelhead Trout with Cherry Tomatoes   134
- Grilled Whole Branzino with Herbs & Loads of Lime   137
- Seared Tuna Steaks with Ponzu, Crispy Garlic & Cucumbers   138
- Flaky Whitefish with Brown Butter Walnut Vinaigrette   141
- Stovetop Miso Halibut en Papillote with Napa Cabbage   142
- Seared Scallops with Dill Chimichurri & White Beans   145
- Grapefruit & Ginger Cured Salmon on Bagels   146
- Crispy-Skinned Salmon with Couscous & Zucchini Tzatziki   149
- Grilled Sumac Shell-On Shrimp   150

Winner, Winner, Chicken Dinner!   152

- Really Good Roast Chicken   155
- Orangey Chicken Piccata with Jammy Shallots   157
- Curried Chicken & Celery Salad Sandwiches   161
- Skillet Hot Sauce & Brown Sugar Chicken Thighs with Frazzled Snap Peas   162
- Aleppo-Braised Chicken Legs with Butter Beans & Smashed Olives   165
- Fajita-Rubbed Chicken with Grilled Bell Peppers   166
- Honey Buffalo Glazed Chicken with Shaved Carrots   169
- Garlic & Old Bay Brick Chicken with Schmaltzy Baby Potatoes   170
- Crispy Sesame & Herb Chicken Schnitzel   173
- Pomegranate Yogurt Marinated Grilled Chicken   174

Meat Me Halfway   176

- Spiced Lamb Meatballs with Feta, Tomato & Cucumber Salad   178
- Onion Butter Kebab Koobideh with Radishes & Herbs   182
- Smash Burgers with Secret Sauce   186
- Steak & Potatoes for Two with Asparagus & Bagna Cauda   189
- Auntie Nina's Spicy Slow-Braised Beef Chitanni   191
- Chitanni, Provolone & Shishito Cheesesteak   195
- Coffee & Cayenne Rubbed Ribs with Mustard Barbecue Sauce   196
- Galbi-Inspired Steak with Quick Pear Kimchi   199
- Black Pepper & Coriander Rack of Lamb with Mint Zhoug & Chickpeas   201

Sides, Vegetables & Things   204

Maple Chili Glazed Carrots with Carrot-Top Salsa Verde   206

Charred Cabbage with Calabrian Chili Butter   209

Shawarma-Spiced Whole Roasted Cauliflower with Garlicky Tahini & Quick-Pickled Onions   210

Pan-Fried Panko-Crusted Eggplant with Jammy Cherry Tomatoes & Burrata   213

Sheet Pan Salt & Pepper Radishes   217

Chili Garlic Brussels Sprouts with Furikake   218

Sour Cream & Caramelized Onion Potatoes   221

Roasted Broccolini with Cilantro-Lime Vinaigrette   222

Pecorino Paprika Polenta Fries   225

Za'atar-Roasted Kabocha Squash with Pomegranate Dressing   226

A Pot o' Rice   228

Lemony Couscous with a Kick   229

Sweets & Treats   230

Tahini Chocolate Chip Cookies with Toasted Sesame Seeds   232

Brown Sugar Hojicha Banana Bread   235

Red Wine–Poached Pears with Vanilla Yogurt & Pistachios   236

Salted Caramel Chocolate Mousse   239

Brown Butter & Miso Cinnamon Babka   241

Individual Mixed-Berry Crumbles   245

Strawberry & Cardamom Mascarpone Puffs   246

Let's Drink, Shall We?   248

Simple Syrup   250

Aperol Mezcal Margarita with Tajín   250

Blackberry Maple Bourbon Old-Fashioned   253

Lime & Basil Gin Sour   254

Mango, Mandarin & Ginger Smoothie with a Tangy Sumac Rim   257

Grandpa's Piping Hot Chai   258

All the Sauces, Dressings & Condiments Your Heart Desires   261

Parties & Pairings   263

Acknowledgments   267

Index   268

What Are We Going to Eat?

Anyone who knows me will tell you I have the same burning question running through my mind every day.

No matter who I am with, it's only a matter of time before I ask: **What are we going to eat?** Inevitably, I respond to my own question and the answer is always the same: **"Something Delicious!"**

As a young girl, I always had my television tuned to the Food Network. I would gaze at the screen, completely focused on the dishes vividly displayed in front of me and I always kept a notebook next to me to jot down all the recipes I would want to explore. My mom didn't have the same passion for cooking that I did, which ultimately turned out in my favor. It meant I was able to practice in our kitchen anytime I wanted since not much was happening there. In many ways her lack of enthusiasm for cooking gave me free rein and endless hours to explore, so I guess she's right when she says that I have her to thank.

My grandma Daisy was the first person who really fostered my love for cooking. While she taught me the fundamentals, she was also the one who embedded in me the interconnectedness of family and food. She taught me that cooking was about being present and using all of our senses, not just when making food but also when enjoying food with company.

Family has certainly played a huge role in my cooking, impacting the way I cook, what I cook, and how I cook. Two of my grandparents grew up in India, but my great-grandparents were raised in Baghdad, the capital of Iraq. My family was part of a small number of Baghdadi Jews living in India since the nineteenth century, and they thought that moving to America would allow for a better life for their new growing family. It is no surprise, then, that much of my cooking reflects my family's heritage, influenced by these countries and beyond. Dishes such as dal, schnitzel, and shakshuka were all staples for me growing up. These were the foods that defined my upbringing and that make me feel comforted, even in the present day.

I come from a large extended family and we are all close, and by close I mean we all live within a half-mile radius of each other. They have all taught me so much about cooking and our culture, and how deeply intertwined the two are. Cooking for the family has been our way of connecting and showing up for each other. It is our way of conveying how much we all care and love one another. The beautiful thing about food and culture is that the learning never ends. I'm constantly discovering new food combinations and styles. In recent years, it's been my husband, Danny, who has introduced me to a new world of cuisines. His Persian roots brought a whole new dimension to my palate, so of course, I included some of my favorites in the book.

Born and raised in Los Angeles, I am also largely influenced by the variety of restaurants and diverse cuisines that LA has to offer. I discovered the value of exploring outside my own heritage and experiencing the richness of the foods from other cultures. It became a source of inspiration, being able to go a short drive to Koreatown to eat Korean BBQ, or driving past taco stands and smelling the corn tortillas heating up on the griddle. I became intrigued with how colors, textures, and sounds play a vital role in eating and cooking.

I continue to cook with a sense of presence whenever I'm in the kitchen. Sound, sight, touch, taste, and smell all play an important role in my cooking process. **Hearing** the sizzling sound of steak hitting a piping-hot pan can help guide your cooking. **Feeling** the textures of kneading dough, or a perfectly cooked chicken breast, can help guide doneness. **Tasting** to your preference, salting your steak, or adding more lemon to your vinaigrettes, allow you to discover your personal palate and preferred flavor profiles. **Smelling** aromatics like garlic as they hit a hot pan can tell you when it's time to add the next ingredient. **Looking** at tomato paste browning signals when it's time to deglaze with wine.

All the resources you need to cook are at your disposal with your senses. Paying attention to them can make the process simple and fun. With minimal equipment, cleanup, and ingredients, my hope is that the recipes in this book will be a helpful resource for you. By applying the techniques and making these recipes your own, you, too, will be able to connect and experience the power of your senses and begin to build your own new memories and cook **something delicious.**

The Recipe for "Something Delicious"

① Read the recipe from head to toe

First things first! Make sure you read the recipe's ingredients, special equipment, and instructions **before** starting prep. Then begin reading through any prep in the ingredient list first (such as chopping your onions or mincing your shallots). Then move on to the instructions. Don't neglect reading the special notes at the bottom, either. There might be a suggested substitute if you don't have an ingredient or an appliance you need, or there may be notes on a technique you are not familiar with, like making a vinaigrette or spatchcocking a chicken (don't worry, we'll get there). Create your plan—this way you can avoid any hiccups, ensuring that the recipe will be simple to execute the first time, and even easier time and time again.

KEY TO RECIPE ICONS

Vegan   Vegetarian   Gluten Free   Dairy free

② Mise en place—"Putting in place"

Mise en place is a French culinary phrase that translates to "putting in place," meaning, prepping and organizing everything you need for a recipe beforehand. The way you set up your cooking station and prepare the ingredients before you begin cooking will determine how successful (or unsuccessful) your final dish will be. Bring out any special equipment needed, such as a stand mixer, blender, or food processor so you're not running around trying to find the lid of your blender (you'll thank me later!). Does the recipe require you to mince, chop, or quarter your onions? Get everything in order first, so when it's time to cook, you can start seamlessly.

③ Scan the recipe for sensory cues

Using your senses allows you to become more present in your cooking and often clears your mind from the noise of the day. By actively using all of your senses—sound, sight, touch, taste, and smell—you will experience cooking in a new light.

 Sound

This might be surprising, but it's important to really tune in while cooking. By becoming silent you'll be able to hear those sizzling or popping sounds that indicate you are on the right track. Sound cues are also important for you to know the perfect time to proceed with the next step of the cooking process: For example, you'll know if you add meat to a hot skillet and it doesn't sizzle, the skillet is not hot enough. Aside from aiding in the actual preparation of the meal, when you allow yourself to fully immerse in the sounds of boiling, mixing, pouring, sizzling, frying, and chopping, together they create a symphony.

Sight

A visually appealing final dish is ultimately what entices you to eat it. The colors and textures we see before digging in are our first impressions. We eat with our eyes first! So, make sure to read through the phrases in the instructions. You will see things like, "Watch for a golden brown hue," "Should be a little glossy," or "Wait for a vibrant green color." Don't skip these steps! Your eyes will thank you.

 ### Touch

Another way to ensure you are heading in the right direction with your recipe is to use the sense of touch. Touching your food can determine your progress. A cake that springs back when lightly poked is a sign of doneness. Using your fingertips to touch a steak can help you achieve your preferred doneness (mine is medium-rare). Mixing with your hands is also the easiest way sometimes! These are ways touch plays an important role in the cooking process.

 ### Taste

Our tongues distinguish different tastes: salty, sweet, sour, bitter, and umami. For example:

> **Salty:** Salt, soy sauce, olives
> **Sweet:** Sugar, honey, maple syrup, agave
> **Sour:** Citrus, vinegar, yogurt
> **Bitter:** Coffee, endive, arugula
> **Umami:** Miso, tomatoes, anchovies

Tasting as you go is the most crucial step in nailing a recipe. It allows you to make adjustments throughout the cooking process. For example, anchovies provide natural saltiness, so you can make the assessment that you may need to level down a tad on the salt. Is your dish *too* salty? You can fix this by adding a sour or sweet element to balance it out.

 ### Smell

Your sense of smell has the power to evoke emotions and nostalgic memories. The aroma of eggplant roasting in the oven takes me back to memories of my dad preparing baba ghanoush for our high holiday family dinners (he is always on baba ghanoush duty!). The aroma of meaty burgers on the grill brings me back to hot, summer days enjoying sunshine.

Smell can also indicate your progress when cooking through a recipe. The toasty smell of walnuts when they hit a hot dry skillet or the scent of spices, like red pepper flakes blooming in olive oil, gives you a hint of what's to come.

You can use recipes as your map, but your senses are your compass when pursuing the best overall outcome for the dish (and helping you nail flavor according to your personal palate). Cooking in this instinctive way allows you to refine and advance your kitchen skills. It is a form of self-expression that makes recipes unique to you.

 ## Get started!

As you begin cooking, the ingredients will be listed in the order of use, allowing you to easily track your progress through each step in the recipe. After reviewing the recipe, checking the ingredients, gathering any necessary special equipment, and familiarizing yourself with the instructions, sensory cues, and preparing your station (mise en place), you are now ready to start.

Let's Cook SOMETHING DELICIOUS!

Shop My Kitchen

There are a number of ingredients I like to have stocked in my pantry and fridge, and below are the items that I buy often to ensure I'm set up for success at all times.

Pantry

Alliums
Garlic
Onions: red, white, yellow
Shallots and musir (dried shallots)

Anchovies

Broths
Beef, chicken, vegetable

Beans and legumes
Butter (lima) beans
Cannellini beans
Chickpeas
Lentils

Citrus
Lemons
Limes
Oranges

Condiments
Chili crisp
Chili oil
Fish sauce
Gochujang
Mirin

Flours and powders
Tipo "00" flour
Active dry yeast
All-purpose flour
Baking powder
Baking soda
Bread flour

Grains and legumes
Couscous: pearl and fine
Farro
Polenta
Quinoa

Rice: basmati and short-grain

Nuts and seeds
Cashews
Hazelnuts
Pecans
Pistachios
Sesame seeds
Walnuts

Oil
Extra-virgin olive oil, for cooking and for finishing
Neutral oil: avocado oil, vegetable oil, canola oil, grapeseed oil
Toasted sesame oil

Panko bread crumbs

Pasta and noodles
Pasta: short-cut and strand
Ramen noodles

Spices, herbs, and extracts
Aleppo pepper
Black peppercorns: freshly ground, cracked, coarse black pepper
Cardamom
Cayenne pepper
Chili powder
Cinnamon: ground, sticks
Cumin, ground
Curry powder
Diamond Crystal kosher salt
Dried oregano
Flaky salt
Furikake
Garam masala
Garlic powder
Gochugaru (Korean chile flakes)
Mustard seeds
Red pepper flakes
Saffron threads
Smoked paprika
Sumac
Togarashi
Turmeric, ground
Vanilla extract
White peppercorns

Sweeteners
Agave
Honey
Maple syrup
Pomegranate molasses
Sugar: dark brown, light brown, granulated

Tomato products
Crushed tomatoes
Diced tomatoes
Fire-roasted tomatoes
Tomato paste
Whole peeled tomatoes

Vinegar
Apple cider vinegar
Balsamic vinegar
Distilled white vinegar
Red wine vinegar
Rice vinegar
Sherry vinegar
White wine vinegar

Wine and liquor
Bourbon
Dry red wine: Shiraz, Pinot, Merlot, or Syrah
Dry white wine: Pinot Grigio, Sauvignon Blanc, or Chardonnay
Gin
Mezcal
Sake
Soju

Fridge

Dairy and eggs
Butter, unsalted
Eggs, large
Yogurt, whole-milk Greek
Heavy cream
Kashk (Persian whey)
Labneh
Milk, whole
Burrata cheese
Parmigiano-Reggiano cheese
Pecorino Romano cheese
Ricotta cheese

Condiments and sauces
Ketchup
Mayonnaise: Kewpie and Hellmann's/Best Foods
Calabrian chili paste
Harissa paste
Miso paste
Mustard: Dijon, yellow, whole-grain
Ponzu
Soy sauce, coconut aminos, tamari
Sriracha, sambal oelek, chili garlic sauce
Tamarind paste

Pickles and olives
Capers
Castelvetrano olives
Kalamata olives
Pepperoncini
Pickled jalapeños

Tools & Tips

Investing in quality cookware will level up your cooking, but don't feel the pressure to get everything all at once. I've spent over a decade collecting and adding pieces to my kitchen, constantly elevating my cooking game. You don't need a lot of equipment either, just a few pieces will go a long way. I recommend the following:

Basics

Blender: A high-powered blender or immersion blender is perfect for soups, purees, smoothies, vinaigrettes, and sauces. I use a large Vitamix for bigger portions, but I also use a smaller Ninja for smaller serving sizes of dressing, smoothies, and sauces.

Cast-iron skillet: I swear by my Lodge cast-iron skillet. I've had my first one for over a decade, and I'm sure I'll have it for way longer. This is one of the most versatile skillets in the kitchen. It can go on the stovetop, oven, and on the grill. I know that washing it may seem daunting, but bear with me, it's not! Give it a scrub with soap and water like a regular skillet, then wipe it off immediately, seasoning with neutral oil to store between paper towels! Don't leave your cast-iron skillet wet or it will rust. A 10- to 12-inch skillet to start should do the trick.

Cutting board: Your workstation is very important. Something that has helped me stay organized in the kitchen is keeping a hefty medium-size wooden cutting board on the counter for all things chopping and prepping (I like a Boos Block!).

Dutch oven: I'll never forget when I got my first Staub Dutch oven, well over a decade ago as well, and it still works like brand new. Opt for a 5- to 8-quart, depending on how many people you usually cook for. This is great for stews, braises, soups, pasta, searing, deep-frying, really anything!

Knives: One of the most important kitchen tools is a good, sharp knife. Start with a 7- to 9-inch chef's knife, a paring knife, and kitchen shears. A serrated knife is also great to have for bread and tomatoes.

Loaf pans: All you need to make any type of loaf, such as cakes or bread, is a 9 by 5-inch loaf pan. The Brown Sugar Hojicha Banana Bread (page 235) and the Brown Butter & Miso Cinnamon Babka (page 241) work well with this size loaf pan.

Sheet pans: A set of quarter-sheet and half-sheet pans will be a life changer when setting up mise en place, roasting veg, cooking proteins in the oven, and making cookies. A 14-inch square pizza pan (I love my LloydPan) is great for Danny's Sicilian Pizza with Garlicky Oil (page 46). You can use this pizza pan for other things like focaccia, cakes, and more.

Stainless steel pans and skillets: When I got my first stainless steel set, it was game over. I love to use a 3-quart saucier for making pasta, soups, and stews, as well as a 10- to 12-inch skillet for searing proteins and toasting nuts. I've had my Made In and All-Clad stainless steel pots and pans for years and they are still in pristine condition. Start with the skillet and saucier, and work your way up to a collection including a 1-quart saucepan, and a large stockpot.

Smaller Tools

These smaller tools are helpful when flipping fish, shredding Parmesan, brushing on simple syrup, rolling out dough, scraping ingredients, or grating garlic.

- Bench scraper with ruler
- Box grater
- Dry and wet measuring spoons and cups
- Fish spatula
- Large tongs
- Microplane
- Pastry brush
- Rolling pin
- Silicone spatulas: small, medium, large
- Spider strainer
- Whisks: small, medium, large
- Wooden spoons: small, medium, large

Nice to Have

Instant-read thermometer: Many of the recipes in this book recommend the use of a thermometer. Using a thermometer will take the guesswork out of cooking, ensuring you get the perfect temp every time.

Nonstick skillet: A nonstick skillet can be used for omelets, pancakes, and crispy-skinned salmon. I like to have an 8- or 10-inch available.

When I call for a skillet in a recipe, unless otherwise specified you can use a nonstick, cast-iron, or stainless steel skillet.

Temperatures for Cooking Proteins

- Chicken: 165°F
- Fish: 135° to 145°F
- Lamb: 125° to 130°F
- Pork: 145° to 165°F
- Steak: medium-rare 125° to 130°F

Colanders and fine-mesh sieves: A small and large colander, and a few small to large sizes of fine-mesh sieves, will help you strain and drain when making sauces, drinks, and pastas.

Cheesecloth: I love to have cheesecloth handy for any sort of straining. It's helpful to have for the Marinated Labneh Balls (page 52) and Kebab Koobideh (page 182).

Cooling rack: As an extension of the sheet pan, I like to use a cooling rack for things like resting steak, cookies, or banana bread.

Deli containers: Get an assortment of sizes. They come in 8-, 12-, 16-, 32-ounce sizes. These are great for prepping and storing, as well as organizing your mise en place.

Digital scale: For the baking recipes in this book, I use a scale to weigh out ingredients and include grams where necessary. You *can* use measuring cups and spoons and it will still turn out great, but to make your baked goods to perfection, I do recommend a scale!

Food processor: Depending on how many servings you typically make, a small or large food processor will help you blitz and pulse at a rapid rate.

Mortar and pestle: I love my mortar and pestle to grind spices, like fennel seeds and peppercorns. I also like to use it for blooming saffron, or for sauces, like pesto or Caesar dressing.

Mixing bowls: Make sure you have small, medium, and large ones on hand. I find that aluminum or glass mixing bowls work best.

Parchment paper: I use parchment paper sheets for wrapping sandwiches, roasting veggies, or roasting chicken, and they're great for easy cleanup.

Stand mixer or hand mixer: Either will work and will help you when baking or making doughs. My KitchenAid stand mixer has been with me for almost two decades and continues to be a powerhouse in the kitchen.

snacks & apps

SERVES 4
45 MINUTES

1 to 1½ pounds chicken wings, a mix of drumettes and flats

1 tablespoon extra-virgin olive oil

Kosher salt and freshly ground black pepper

Grated zest of 1 small Meyer lemon, plus 1 tablespoon fresh Meyer lemon juice

1 tablespoon harissa paste

1 teaspoon honey

2 tablespoons unsalted butter

If you can't find Meyer lemons, sub with any lemon available (or you can always join me in my parents' backyard!)

Serve with Gorgonzola Dressing (page 76) or Ranch-ish Dressing (page 84) for dipping.

MEYER LEMON & HARISSA WINGS

I grew up with a huge Meyer lemon tree in our backyard and loved pulling lemons off the tree whenever I wanted. To this day when citrus is in season, I head over to my parents' backyard and load up a huge bag. Meyer lemons are sweet, floral, and not as acidic as other lemons. The sweetness works nicely with harissa paste, a spicy hot chile pepper paste from Africa, oftentimes used in Middle Eastern cooking. This lemony, spicy sauce is tossed with chicken wings (you can either grill or bake!) making this a tangy appetizer for any occasion.

1. **If baking:** Arrange racks in the upper and lower thirds of the oven and preheat your oven to 425°F. Line a sheet pan with parchment paper.
If grilling: Preheat your grill to medium-high heat for two-zone cooking.

2. Pat the wings dry with paper towels. **If baking:** Put the wings on the lined sheet pan and toss them with the olive oil and salt and pepper. Arrange the wings in a single layer with the skin-side down. **If grilling:** In a bowl, toss the wings with the olive oil, salt, and pepper.

3. **To bake:** Transfer the sheet pan to the bottom rack of the oven and bake for 20 minutes. Flip the wings over, transfer to the top rack, and continue to bake until golden brown, crisp, and fully cooked through, 20 to 25 minutes.

4. **To grill:** Place the wings skin-side down on the cooler, indirect heat side of the grill, cover, and cook for 20 minutes. Flip the wings over. Your wings should have darkened in color slightly and cooked through. Transfer to the hot side of the grill to get a nice crust and char to crisp your wings, 5 to 8 minutes, flipping halfway. Depending on the heat of your grill, you can go up to 10 to 12 minutes, flipping halfway through, to get your preferred char and the internal temperature of your wings reaches 165°F.

5. **Make your lemon & harissa sauce:** While your wings are in the oven or on the grill, in a large saucepan, whisk together the lemon zest, lemon juice, harissa paste, honey, and salt and pepper to taste. Set on the stovetop or the cooler side of the grill and heat until just warmed through. Move off the heat and add the butter, whisking until melted and combined.

6. **To serve:** Once your wings are cooked, transfer them to the large saucepan with the lemon & harissa sauce, tossing until completely combined. Transfer to a serving platter to serve.

SERVES 4
30 MINUTES

AHI TUNA AGUACHILE VERDE WITH TOSTADAS

¼ cup thinly sliced red onion

6 corn tortillas (store-bought tostadas work as a shortcut)

2 teaspoons extra-virgin olive oil, plus more for brushing and drizzling

1 serrano chile

1 bunch of fresh cilantro, roughly chopped (including stems), plus cilantro sprigs for garnish

2 large garlic cloves, peeled but whole

½ cup fresh lime juice (3 to 4 large)

2 tablespoons ice water

1 tablespoon agave nectar or granulated sugar

Pinch of kosher salt

1 large English cucumber, peeled, halved lengthwise, seeded, and cut into half-moons

1 large avocado, diced

1 pound sushi-grade ahi tuna, cut into ½-inch cubes

Freshly ground black pepper

Serve with Aperol Mezcal Margarita with Tajín (page 250).

My first experience with aguachile was in Mexico, on our annual family trip where our diet consisted of raw seafood. Aguachile, originating from Sinaloa, Mexico, is a dish traditionally made of shrimp, tossed with a blend of chile and lime juice. It quickly became a favorite of mine. The sauce is spicy, tangy, earthy, acidic, and super lime-forward—there is nothing *not* to love. For this variation, I'm using ahi tuna and serving it alongside some crunchy tostadas.

1. **Equipment:** Bring out your stand blender.

2. Place your thinly sliced red onion in a large bowl and cover with cool water and set aside. This reduces pungency and crisps it up.

3. **Make your tostadas:** Preheat your oven to 400°F or an air fryer to 350°F.

4. On a baking sheet (or air fryer basket) lay out your corn tortillas and use a brush or paper towel to grease them with olive oil. Crisp up for 8 to 10 minutes in the oven or 4 to 5 minutes in the air fryer. Remove from the oven or air fryer and set aside.

5. **Make your aguachile sauce:** Roughly chop half of your serrano pepper (remove the seeds if you prefer it less spicy). Thinly slice the other half and set aside for garnish. In a blender, combine the chopped serrano, cilantro, garlic, lime juice, ice water, agave nectar, and salt. Blend until smooth and well combined. Season to taste with salt. Set aside in the fridge.

6. **Prepare your tuna:** Drain your red onions from the large bowl and pat dry. Return to the large bowl and add the cucumber, avocado, ahi tuna, 2 teaspoons olive oil, and salt and black pepper to taste. Toss softly until combined.

7. **Assemble the dish:** In two shallow dishes meant for sharing, layer in half of your aguachile sauce. Then add half of the ahi mixture, placing it on top and shaping it into a little upright tower. Not only does this look really beautiful, but adding the mixture on top instead of tossing it all together prevents discoloration from the acid of the sauce.

8. Garnish with the cilantro sprigs, thinly sliced serrano, a drizzle of olive oil, and black pepper. Serve with your baked tostadas.

SERVES 4
30 MINUTES

2 tablespoons extra-virgin olive oil

2 tablespoons honey

2 teaspoons curry powder

2 teaspoons turbinado sugar

1½ teaspoons Diamond Crystal kosher salt

¼ teaspoon cracked black pepper

2 cups mixed raw nuts, such as pistachios, cashews, walnuts, pecans

¼ cup pumpkin seeds

CURRY & HONEY SPICED NUTS

A party is never complete without a salty, sweet, and crunchy nut mix. We all need something to snack on while we wait for dinner, and this is the perfect opener. This could be served alongside a gorg charcuterie or cheese board. This would also work on top of ice cream, yogurt, or boxed as a hostess gift! These spiced assorted nuts are tossed with turbinado sugar, curry powder, and honey, bringing out an earthy aroma and a crunchy sweetness of flavor.

1. Preheat your oven to 350°F. Line a sheet pan with parchment paper.

2. In a medium bowl, stir together the olive oil, honey, curry powder, turbinado sugar, salt, and black pepper. Add your mixed nuts and pumpkin seeds and toss until completely incorporated. Pour onto your sheet pan, separating the nuts and pumpkin seeds in an even layer.

3. Bake until the nuts and seeds are fragrant and turn a nice toasty brown, 15 to 20 minutes, stirring halfway through.

4. Let the mixture cool for a couple of minutes on the sheet pan to get its crunch and crisp back. Serve warm or at room temperature or transfer to an airtight container and store for up to 3 days.

SERVES 4
1 HOUR

ICY CRUDITÉS WITH ROASTED GARLIC TARRAGON YOGURT DIP

2 large heads garlic

2 teaspoons extra-virgin olive oil, plus more for drizzling

Kosher salt

1 cup whole-milk Greek yogurt

2 tablespoons finely chopped fresh tarragon

Grated zest of ½ small lemon, plus 1 tablespoon fresh lemon juice

Freshly ground black pepper

Your favorite vegetables, such as radishes, cucumber, carrots, endive, cut for dipping

Crushed ice, for serving

If you're in a pinch or don't want to wait to roast garlic, sub in 2 raw garlic cloves, minced.

This dip will have your friends and family comin' back for more. The depth of flavor from the roasted garlic is unexpected, and absolutely perfect with the tangy yogurt and fresh tarragon. Any other herbs will do, too, like dill or parsley. Serve with your favorite veg (I like radishes and cucumber). Add crushed ice to your veggies to keep everything cool and crunchy.

1. **Roast your garlic:** Preheat your oven to 400°F. Cut off the tops of the garlic heads to expose the cloves. Place the garlic heads on a piece of aluminum foil, drizzle with 1 teaspoon of the olive oil, and sprinkle with a pinch of salt. Wrap the garlic tightly in the foil and place on a baking sheet. Roast until the garlic cloves are soft and golden brown, 40 to 45 minutes. Remove from the oven and let cool slightly.

2. Once the roasted garlic is cool enough to handle, squeeze the cloves out of their skins into a medium bowl. Mash the garlic with a fork until you have a smooth paste.

3. **Make the dip:** To the mashed garlic, add the Greek yogurt, tarragon, lemon zest, lemon juice, remaining 1 teaspoon olive oil, and salt and black pepper to taste. Toss and mix well to combine completely.

4. **To serve:** Transfer the dip to a serving bowl, drizzle with some olive oil, and season with a crank of freshly ground black pepper. Set your dip and favorite vegetables on a platter and fill the space around the bowl with crushed ice. Serve immediately.

SERVES 6
1 HOUR 30 MINUTES

2 tablespoons unsalted butter

2 large yellow onions, thinly sliced into half-moons

2 large shallots, thinly sliced into half-moons

Kosher salt and freshly ground black pepper

5 large garlic cloves, minced

1 bunch of scallions, finely chopped

¼ cup finely chopped fresh chives, plus more for garnish

2 tablespoons balsamic vinegar

½ cup sour cream

¼ cup mayonnaise

2 ounces salmon roe

Crinkle-cut potato chips, for serving

Vegetarian option: Omit the salmon roe.

CARAMELIZED FIVE-ALLIUM DIP TOPPED WITH SALMON ROE

I grew up on Lipton Onion Soup Mix and Trader Joe's Caramelized Onion Dip. Given that my mom is not a cook by any means (her words, not mine . . . okay, mine, too), she would serve the onion soup mix tossed with sour cream as a dip with chips nightly as a snack before dinner, and sometimes *for* dinner. Therefore, I consider myself an expert when it comes to onion dip! (Thanks, Mom!)

With five types of caramelized alliums, this appetizer is my ode to both of those special dips, which, honestly, kept me alive. Here I top it off with salmon roe and serve with crinkle-cut potato chips. The salmon roe is an easy addition to this childhood staple and makes the young gal in me feel quite fancy.

1. **Caramelize the alliums:** In a medium skillet, heat the butter over medium heat until melted and glistening. Add your onions and shallots, tossing to coat evenly with the melted butter. Season with salt and black pepper to taste. Sweat (which means softening your onions without allowing any browning) for 10 minutes, stirring occasionally until your onions and shallots are glistening and translucent.

2. Reduce the heat to medium-low and continue cooking gently, stirring often, until very soft and golden, 10 to 15 minutes more. You want this low and slow, so you shouldn't hear any loud sizzling—adjust the heat as needed to keep it from browning too quickly. As you see browning on your onions and shallots, adjust by tossing them with a tablespoon or two of water, to deglaze the pan periodically as you caramelize.

3. Crank up the heat to medium and add your garlic, scallions, chives, and balsamic vinegar, plus more salt and black pepper to taste. Caramelize for another 10 minutes on low heat and let all the alliums get dark in color. When fully caramelized (they should be sticky, jammy, and medium-brown at this point), remove from the heat and cool slightly, about 5 minutes.

4. **Make the dip:** Add your sour cream and mayonnaise to the skillet. Toss to combine, seasoning to taste. Transfer to a medium bowl, cover, and store in the fridge for at least 30 minutes to chill and allow the flavors to meet each other.

5. **To serve:** Garnish the dip with chopped chives and finish with salmon roe. Serve with crinkle-cut potato chips.

SERVES 4
30 MINUTES

PERSIAN SHALLOT DIP WITH SUMAC & SAFFRON CHILI CRISP

SUMAC & SAFFRON CHILI CRISP

¼ teaspoon saffron threads

1 cup grapeseed oil

2 large shallots, thinly sliced into rings, rings separated

4 large garlic cloves, thinly sliced

1 tablespoon sumac

1 tablespoon red pepper flakes

1 tablespoon gochugaru (Korean chile flakes)

1 teaspoon Diamond Crystal kosher salt

1 teaspoon granulated sugar

1½ teaspoons toasted sesame seeds

PERSIAN SHALLOT DIP

½ cup musir (Persian dried shallots, see note) or ¼ cup finely chopped shallots

1 cup labneh or whole-milk Greek yogurt

½ teaspoon dried mint

Kosher salt and freshly ground black pepper

This Persian dip, also known as *mast-o musir*, is a dried shallot dip tossed with mint. (*Mast* means "yogurt" and *musir* means "shallots.") The dried shallots are rehydrated in water and give off a sweet onion flavor. When I go out for Persian food, this is what I'm ordering, and if I'm making Persian food at home, this is what I'm serving alongside Kebab Koobideh (page 182).

A traditional dip with an untraditional twist: I had a dream about a sumac and saffron chili combo, and rushed to the kitchen the next day to test it out. You get the aromatic scent from the saffron, the nuttiness and citrus smell from the sumac, and all the spice from the assorted chiles. You also get the yummy crunch from the shallots and garlic. This is then drizzled all around the mast-o musir, and similar to the Caramelized Five-Allium Dip (page 29), this one works extremely well with crinkle-cut chips.

1. **Make your Sumac & Saffron Chili Crisp:** First, bloom your saffron. In a mortar and pestle, grind your saffron into a pasty powder. (If you don't have a mortar and pestle, just grind between your fingers and place in a cup.) Add 2 small ice cubes or 1 tablespoon ice water to the mortar (or the cup). Allow the ice to melt completely, which will bloom your saffron, adding flavor, aroma, and color; it should be a vibrant, almost electric orange. Now you have your saffron water!

2. Line a plate with paper towels and have near the stove. In a medium saucepan, combine the oil and shallots and set over medium-high heat. Stir frequently until the shallots are lightly golden, 4 to 6 minutes. Add your garlic and cook until the shallots are crisp and the garlic is lightly golden, 1 to 2 minutes.

3. Use a slotted spoon or a spider strainer to transfer your crispy shallots and garlic to the paper towels to cool completely and drain off any excess oil. Turn off the heat but keep your oil on the stovetop.

4. To the oil in the saucepan, add the sumac, red pepper flakes, gochugaru, salt, and sugar. Toss to combine and allow your spices to bloom in the warmed oil for 1 to 2 minutes.

You can find musir at most Middle Eastern and Persian Markets, it's also available for order on Amazon. If you can't find musir, you can substitute with regular fresh shallots.

5. Remove the pan from the stovetop and add your bloomed saffron water, sesame seeds, shallots, and garlic. Give it a big toss and allow it to cool completely before transferring it to a jar with a tight cover. You can store the chili crisp at room temperature for up to 1 month or in the fridge for 3 months.

6. **Make your Persian Shallot Dip:** Place the musir in hot water to cover until rehydrated, about 10 minutes, and until the hot water has cooled. Drain and pat dry. You want some crunch on the shallots, so you are not looking for a super softened texture here. Cut around to discard any darker, porous, parts on the musir. Mince finely with your knife until you almost have a paste. You can also use a Microplane or other grater to do this. This will take a moment, so take your time to ensure they are finely minced!

7. **To serve:** In a medium bowl, toss together your musir, labneh, mint, and salt and black pepper to taste. Set aside in the fridge until you are ready to serve. Spread the dip in a bowl, finishing with a drizzling of 1 tablespoon Sumac & Saffron Chili Crisp.

SERVES 4
45 MINUTES

CRISPY TEMPURA CAULIFLOWER TOSSED IN SPICY MISO MAYO

You've likely seen a rendition of this dish at most sushi restaurants, perhaps with shrimp (the Rock Shrimp Tempura with Yuzu at Nobu is a game changer). This version consists of tender, soft cauliflower coated with an airy and light tempura batter, and then tossed with spicy miso mayo. It's the perfect starter for any meal—or turn it into a main by serving it alongside white rice.

TEMPURA CAULIFLOWER

½ cup all-purpose flour

⅔ cup seltzer water

1 large egg yolk

¼ teaspoon togarashi (see note)

Kosher salt and freshly ground black pepper

1 medium head cauliflower

Neutral oil, for deep-frying

SPICY MISO MAYO

¼ cup mayonnaise, preferably Kewpie Japanese mayonnaise

2 tablespoons finely chopped fresh chives, plus more for serving

1 tablespoon sriracha, sambal oelek, or chili garlic sauce

1 tablespoon white miso paste

1 teaspoon toasted sesame oil

1 teaspoon distilled white vinegar

½ teaspoon togarashi, plus more for serving

Freshly ground black pepper

Lemon wedges, for squeezing

Togarashi is a spicy Japanese seasoning blend, made with chile peppers, sesame seeds, ginger, citrus peel, and nori. It adds a slightly spicy, tangy, and sweet flavor to this recipe.

1. **Prepare your tempura cauliflower:** In a medium bowl, whisk together the flour, seltzer, egg yolk, togarashi, and salt and black pepper until a smooth batter forms. Look for a pancake batter consistency. Trust the process, it's a wet batter and it will crisp up beautifully. Set the batter aside in the fridge for up to 15 minutes.

2. Cut the cauliflower into bite-size florets, discarding the tough stems. Season with salt to taste and toss to combine.

3. Pour a few inches of neutral oil into a large pot and heat on your stovetop over medium-high heat to 350°F. Line a sheet pan with paper towels and set near the stovetop.

4. **Make your Spicy Miso Mayo:** While your oil is heating, in a large bowl, whisk together the mayonnaise, chives, sriracha, miso, sesame oil, vinegar, togarashi, and black pepper to taste until well combined. Set aside.

5. **Fry the cauliflower:** Dip the cauliflower florets into the tempura batter, coating them evenly. Working in batches to avoid overcrowding, carefully place the battered cauliflower into the hot oil. Fry until the cauliflower is crisp and turns a nice pale golden color, 2 to 4 minutes. You can test doneness by inserting a knife or fork into the cauliflower pieces; it should give just a little bit of resistance.

6. Remove the fried cauliflower using a slotted spoon or tongs and transfer to the paper towels in a single layer to drain any excess oil. Season with salt.

7. **To serve:** Transfer your fried cauliflower to the large bowl with the spicy miso mayonnaise. Toss gently to evenly coat all the cauliflower. Arrange in a serving dish and garnish with chopped chives and a sprinkle of togarashi. Serve with lemon wedges for squeezing.

SERVES 4 TO 6
15 MINUTES

SCALLOP & RADISH CRUDO WITH CHILE & CITRUS

4 medium radishes, preferably watermelon radishes

1 pound sushi-grade sea scallops

2 tablespoons extra-virgin olive oil

Grated zest of 1 large lemon, 2 tablespoons fresh lemon juice, plus thinly sliced lemon peel, for garnish (optional)

Grated zest of ½ small orange, plus 2 tablespoons fresh orange juice

Kosher salt and freshly ground black pepper

½ teaspoon gochugaru or red pepper flakes

If you can't find watermelon radishes, any radish variety will do!

Crudo, which means "raw," is one of those dishes I can never get enough of. Pair it with crunchy radish, loads of fresh punchy citrus juice, and a pinch of gochugaru, and we're in business. The gochugaru, which are Korean chile flakes, adds a nice subtle kick of heat and sweetness. It's a simple yet showstopping plate that is as gorgeous as it is delicious.

1. Thinly slice your radishes ¼ inch thick and place them in a bowl of ice water for at least 5 minutes, and then dry with paper towels.

2. Clean your scallops by removing the side muscle particle sticking out. Just take your finger and pull it off the scallop and discard. Slice your scallops horizontally into ¼-inch-thick discs. Arrange them on a medium to large platter. Nestle the sliced radishes in between the scallops.

3. In a small bowl, combine the olive oil, half of the lemon zest, the lemon juice, orange zest, orange juice, and salt and black pepper to taste. Stir well to combine.

4. Pour the sauce over the scallops and radishes, making sure to distribute evenly across all the scallops and radishes. Finish with a pinch of gochugaru or red pepper flakes and the remaining lemon zest. Garnish with thinly sliced lemon peel over the top (if using).

SERVES 6 TO 8
45 MINUTES

PONZU & TOGARASHI-MARINATED OLIVES

1 cup pitted Castelvetrano olives, drained

1 cup pitted Kalamata olives, drained

1 cup stuffed Manzanilla olives, drained

6 large garlic cloves, thinly sliced, plus more to taste

¼ cup ponzu (I love the Mizkan Ajipon brand, see note)

2 tablespoons toasted sesame oil

1 tablespoon toasted sesame seeds

1 teaspoon togarashi

Ponzu is a Japanese condiment often made from bonito flakes, soy sauce, and yuzu juice, a type of citrus.

Classic marinated olives are a common app, but how about amping up the flavors with ponzu and togarashi? By marinating your olives with ponzu, a Japanese citrus sauce, and togarashi, a Japanese spice blend, you get a citrusy bite with a li'l kick. Castelvetrano olives are my personal favorite because they are super creamy with an almost butter-like finish. They make a great trio with the brininess of the Kalamata and Manzanilla olives.

In a large bowl, combine the olives and garlic. Add the ponzu sauce, sesame oil, toasted sesame seeds, and togarashi. Toss everything until your olives and garlic are coated completely. Cover tightly and set aside at room temperature for at least 30 minutes. Give it another mix before serving, or store in the refrigerator for up to 5 days.

BREADS & SPREADS

SERVES 4
30 MINUTES

One 8-ounce wheel Brie

2 tablespoons strawberry preserves

1 tablespoon chili crisp or Sumac & Saffron Chili Crisp (page 32)

Crusty baguette

2 tablespoons extra-virgin olive oil

CHILI CRISP & STRAWBERRY BAKED BRIE

Who says entertaining needs to be time-consuming? With only three ingredients, this sweet baked Brie with strawberry preserves is a low-effort, high-reward combo. The chili crisp adds the perfect kick of heat. Bake until melted for a soft gooey texture, then spread on a toasted baguette slice. Dip and repeat.

1. Position racks in the top and bottom thirds of the oven and preheat your oven to 350°F. Line a small baking sheet with parchment paper to catch any potential spillage from the cheese.

2. Score your Brie by making parallel cuts ½ inch apart across the top of the rind, not cutting too deep into the cheese. Turn the cheese 90 degrees and do the same thing to make perpendicular cuts.

3. Place the Brie in a baking dish, preferably a round one just large enough to fit the Brie (a 6-inch skillet or dish would work) and place it on the lined baking sheet. Spoon the preserves and chili crisp on top.

4. Bake the Brie on the top rack until loose and not hard to the touch when pressed with a spoon, 15 to 20 minutes. Any longer than 20 minutes, it may get hard, tough, and stringy, and won't be melty.

5. Halfway through the Brie baking, slice your baguette into ½-inch-thick rounds. Arrange the baguette slices on a large baking sheet lined with parchment paper and drizzle with the olive oil. Bake on the bottom rack until toasted, 8 to 10 minutes.

6. Let the Brie cool for 2 to 3 minutes, then serve alongside your toasted crostini.

SERVES 4
30 MINUTES

1 pound baby bella (cremini) mushrooms

8 tablespoons (1 stick/4 ounces) unsalted butter, at room temperature

½ cup minced fresh flat-leaf parsley

4 small or 2 large garlic cloves, finely minced or grated

Kosher salt and freshly ground black pepper

Crusty baguette, for serving

MUSHROOM "ESCARGOTS" WITH PARSLEY BUTTER

If I'm at a French restaurant and escargots (snails) are on the menu, I will be ordering them, without hesitation! Inspired by the classic French escargots, I've made an easy mushroom, non-snail version for home. A very garlicky parsley compound butter is stuffed into mushrooms and roasted (and then broiled!) in the oven. The butter melts so beautifully, leaving a delicious pool of garlic butter to sop up with your crusty baguette. The flavors and aroma are extremely reminiscent of the classic. Use any extra compound butter (or make more to have stored) for other roasted veg or steak! You will feel as if you've been transported to a French bistro in Paris.

1. Position racks in the top and bottom thirds of the oven and preheat your oven to 400°F.

2. Clean your mushrooms by using a paper towel to rub off any dirt on them, no need to wash them with water. Gently tug at the mushroom stems to pull them out, and save the stems for sautéing or stock. Arrange the mushrooms cap-side down in a single layer in a medium baking dish. I don't recommend putting this on a sheet pan because you want to contain all the juices for dipping.

3. In a medium bowl, mix together your softened butter, parsley, garlic, and salt and pepper to taste. Mix extremely well until completely incorporated. (You can also use a food processor if preferred.)

4. With a small spoon, carefully stuff each mushroom cap with some butter. It doesn't need to be perfect, and some can be spilling over with butter (that will be perfect for extra bread dipping!).

5. Roast the mushrooms on the top oven rack for 15 minutes. When the mushrooms have about 5 minutes to go, turn the oven to high broil and broil for 3 to 5 minutes. Keep an eye on this, you want to see some browning on your mushrooms, and the parsley should turn a darker green, with all the butter melted completely.

6. At the same time on the bottom rack, warm the uncut baguette for 4 to 5 minutes, until slightly toasted and soft inside, and remove the bread from the oven.

7. Remove the mushrooms from the oven and let them cool for 1 to 2 minutes. Serve alongside your warm, crusty baguette. Tear off pieces of baguette and dip them in the dish where the butter has melted.

SERVES 6
31 HOURS

DANNY'S SICILIAN PIZZA WITH GARLICKY OIL

After coming back from our first trip to New York, my husband, Danny, was hooked on pizza. Not only did we try over seven pizza places on our short visit, but he took a huge liking to making homemade pizza dough. We now eat pizza twice a week (or more) both at Los Angeles restaurants and at home prepared by my personal pizza chef (Danny).

While a slice from a pie made in a pizza oven is special in its own right, I've personally become excited about Italian pan pizzas, specifically Sicilian. A Sicilian pie, also called *sfincione*, is similar to a fluffy focaccia.

This recipe is New York–style Sicilian, which is different from an Italian Sicilian because traditionally sfincione has bread crumbs and anchovies. Unlike other pizzas, the Sicilian is very tomato-forward, with the tomato sauce being added *after* the cheese, making this super saucy.

Danny's recipe calls for both tipo "00" and bread flours, a combination that adds a nice crunch, fluff, and spring to the dough. He also calls for a mix of low-moisture *and* fresh mozzarella. Amping up with a garlicky oil (pulling inspiration from a grandma-style pie) adds an unexpected burst of flavor. Pizza has become a special tradition for us, so I am excited for you to welcome Danny's much-perfected Sicilian into your home.

PIZZA DOUGH

1½ cups (340g) cold water, preferably filtered or bottled

1 teaspoon (3g) instant dry yeast

2 cups (250g) bread flour

2 cups (250g) tipo "00" flour

1 tablespoon (13g) Diamond Crystal kosher salt

2 teaspoons (6.5g) granulated sugar

¼ cup (40g) extra-virgin olive oil, plus more for proofing and prepping the pan

PIZZA SAUCE, CHEESE & GARLICKY OIL

One 28-ounce can whole peeled tomatoes

¾ teaspoon granulated sugar

Kosher salt and freshly ground black pepper

One 6-ounce block low-moisture whole-milk mozzarella cheese or presliced low-moisture whole-milk mozzarella

6 ounces fresh mozzarella cheese

2 tablespoons extra-virgin olive oil

2 large garlic cloves, grated

2 tablespoons freshly grated Pecorino Romano cheese, plus more to taste

continued...

1. **Equipment:** Get out your stand mixer and snap on the dough hook.

2. **Make your Pizza Dough:** In the bowl of the stand mixer, lightly stir together the cold water and instant yeast until incorporated.

3. Separately, in a large bowl, combine the bread flour, "00" flour, salt, and sugar. Danny lightly whisks using a fork to incorporate all the dry ingredients for a few seconds.

4. With your stand mixer on low speed, slowly start to add your dry ingredients into the water and yeast, a large spoonful at a time. Keep the mixer on low until the flour is incorporated into a single dough, 3 to 4 minutes. Halfway through, scrape down the sides of the bowl with a silicone spatula. It shouldn't be wet, but it's okay if it's a tad sticky. If you're kneading by hand, knead for 6 to 7 minutes, or until fully combined. (Reserve your large bowl when all the dry ingredients have been added, and set aside.)

DANNY'S SICILIAN PIZZA WITH GARLICKY OIL
continued

5. Turn off your mixer and gently pour the olive oil over the dough in the stand mixer. Do not mix yet; let the dough relax at room temperature in the stand mixer for 10 minutes. This will allow the gluten to relax before the next step.

6. After 10 minutes, put your mixer back on low for 30 seconds to incorporate the olive oil.

7. Remove your dough from the stand mixer and transfer it to your countertop or flat surface. Just drop it on there as is, there's no need to make a ball here. Cover completely with the large bowl you reserved. Let this sit, covered, for 1 hour at room temperature.

8. After 1 hour, form your dough into a ball. Tightly pack it by cupping your hand and gently pulling at the top of the dough and stretching it on all sides toward the bottom of the dough, creating a ball. This should make about one 30-ounce dough ball.

9. Coat the same large bowl with a drizzle more of olive oil, add your ball to the bowl, and turn to coat in the oil. Cover your bowl tightly with a cover or plastic wrap, and transfer to the fridge for 12 to 24 hours; 24 hours is preferable. Your dough should double in size.

10. Take out your dough and leave it covered, letting it sit for 1 hour at room temperature. After an hour, spread about 2 tablespoons of olive oil evenly on the bottom of a 14 by 14-inch pan (Danny prefers a LloydPan), using a paper towel, your hands, or a brush. It should be enough to cover the bottom part of the pan and glisten, this will help to keep your undercarriage of the dough from sticking to the pan so it can get nice and crispy.

11. Transfer your dough to the middle of the pan. Press from the center out, without breaking the dough, and spread gently until it pulls back, with light force. Let this sit for 1 hour in the pan, covered, at room temperature.

12. Gently spread your dough toward the corners of the pan, being careful not to make any holes. At this point, your dough should easily be relaxed enough to press the dough toward the edge of the pan without it springing back. If it's not, allow it to sit for an additional 30 minutes at room temperature. Use your fingers to tap and spread your dough, making divots with your fingers to dimple the dough, like you would with a focaccia.

13. Once your dough fills the pan, let it sit again for another 2 to 3 hours, covered, at room temperature. The longer you wait at room temperature, the more bouncy and fluffy your pizza will get, so be patient!

14. Equipment: While your dough is finishing up resting, get out your stand blender.

15. Make your Pizza Sauce: In the blender, combine the canned whole tomatoes with their liquid, sugar, and salt and pepper to taste and blend until fully combined. Set aside.

16. Shred your cheese: Use a box grater to slice your low-moisture mozzarella cheese into sheets, or thinly slice with a knife or mandoline. Drain your fresh mozzarella, then dry with a towel or paper towel to remove as much moisture as possible. Tear the cheese into small pieces with your hands. As you tear your fresh mozzarella, transfer it to a dry towel to drain further until ready to assemble.

17. Make your Garlicky Oil: In a small bowl, mix together the olive oil, grated garlic, and salt to taste.

18. Now, it is *finally* time to bake your pizza! Position racks in the top and bottom thirds of the oven and preheat your oven to 450°F.

19. Smear ½ cup of your tomato sauce evenly around the pizza dough all the way to the edges. Transfer to the bottom rack to parbake until the bottom of the crust is toasted but not browned and the top of the crust is firm, 10 to 15 minutes. You don't want any char at this point, just a super light toast.

20. Top your pizza: Remove from the oven and arrange the sliced mozzarella and the torn mozzarella evenly across the pizza. Dollop 1½ cups of your tomato sauce over the top of the cheese in your pattern of choice (Danny's favorite is diagonal lines of sauce). Add more if you like it really saucy. You might not use all the sauce.

21. Transfer your pizza now to the top rack in the oven, rotating your pan 180 degrees from the position it was in on the bottom rack, and cook until the bottom of the pizza is browned, your cheese is melted and bubbling, and the top outer crusts of the pizza have turned a golden brown color, 10 to 12 minutes. If you want a little bit more char, or color on your cheese, broil for a few minutes before removing from the oven.

22. Remove from the oven and drizzle with your garlicky oil. Return to the oven for 1 to 2 minutes, to just warm up, until the garlic is fragrant.

23. Remove from the oven and finish with grated Pecorino Romano cheese. Carefully remove from the pan and transfer to a wire rack to cool for at least 5 minutes before transferring to a cutting board and cutting into squares.

Serve with Little Gem Caesar Salad with Habanero Dressing & Sourdough Bread Crumbs (page 71).

MAKES 18 LABNEH BALLS
2 DAYS AND 15 MINUTES

2 cups whole-milk Greek yogurt

1 teaspoon Diamond Crystal kosher salt

1 teaspoon Aleppo pepper

1 teaspoon harissa powder

½ cup extra-virgin olive oil

½ cup grapeseed oil

Fluffy pita bread, for serving

MARINATED LABNEH BALLS WITH HARISSA & ALEPPO PEPPER

Making homemade labneh might seem like a daunting task, but you'd be surprised at how easy it is. If you've never had labneh before, it is a popular Middle Eastern drained yogurt that is sometimes served rolled in balls marinated in oil. It offers a spreadable texture with a delicious blend of sourness and creaminess. All it takes is draining yogurt and a little patience. Don't rush the draining process; the longer the yogurt drains, the thicker and creamier the end result will be. Serve alongside some warm fluffy pita bread. Trust me, it's worth it!

1. **Equipment:** Get out a fine-mesh sieve and some cheesecloth. Line the sieve with the cheesecloth (or use a kitchen towel if you don't have cheesecloth).

2. In a large bowl, combine the Greek yogurt and salt. Stir until the salt is fully incorporated into the yogurt. Transfer the yogurt mixture to the lined sieve and place it over the same large bowl. Gather the edges of the cheesecloth and tie them together, creating a pouch with the yogurt inside. Place a heavy can or weight on top of the pouch to gently press the yogurt.

3. Place the bowl with the sieve in the refrigerator and let the yogurt drain for 2 days.

4. Open up the yogurt mixture; it should be a super-thick consistency. Use your hands to form the mixture into balls, about 1 tablespoon each. You can use some olive oil on your hands if the labneh feels too sticky.

5. In a shallow bowl or rimmed plate, stir together the Aleppo pepper and harissa powder, shaking it into an even layer. Add the labneh balls and shake the dish gently to coat them evenly in the spice mixture. Place them in an airtight container or mason jar, filling it up with olive oil and grapeseed oil, ensuring the balls are fully submerged.

6. Serve right away by spreading the labneh balls on fluffy pita bread, or you can store in the fridge for up to 5 days until ready to serve.

SERVES 4
30 MINUTES

PANZANELLA TOAST WITH SAMBAL AIOLI

PANZANELLA TOAST

2 cups cherry tomatoes, halved

2 Persian cucumbers, finely diced (about ½ cup)

1 small red onion, minced

2 tablespoons extra-virgin olive oil, plus more (optional) for toasting

2 teaspoons distilled white vinegar

Kosher salt and freshly ground black pepper

12 large fresh basil leaves, chiffonade-cut

4 slices (½ inch thick) crusty bread (I like sesame seed sourdough)

SAMBAL AIOLI

½ cup mayonnaise, preferably Kewpie Japanese mayonnaise

2 tablespoons sambal oelek or chili garlic sauce, or less if you prefer less spicy

1 teaspoon distilled white vinegar

1 large garlic clove, grated

Kosher salt and freshly ground black pepper

Summer tomatoes are unbeatable. As soon as I see some ruby red tomatoes (of any kind) my mind immediately goes to panzanella, a Tuscan and Umbrian bread salad tossed with tomatoes, basil, and sometimes cucumbers and red onions. Taking inspiration from the classic panzanella salad, I'm building on an open-faced toast with a chili aioli using sambal oelek, an Indonesian chili sauce. The spice and tang from the mayonnaise are the perfect accompaniment to the juicy tomatoes, fragrant basil, and crunchy cucumbers.

1. **Make your Panzanella Toast:** In a medium bowl, combine the cherry tomatoes, cucumbers, and onion. Add your olive oil, vinegar, and a pinch of salt and black pepper. Gently toss the mixture to coat the ingredients evenly. Add the basil and gently toss to incorporate. Set aside at room temperature.

2. Toast your bread in a toaster or heat a skillet over medium with a drizzle of olive oil and toast the bread slices until they're crispy and golden brown.

3. **Make your Sambal Aioli:** In a small bowl, mix together the mayonnaise, sambal oelek, vinegar, garlic, and salt and pepper to taste.

4. **To assemble:** Spread a generous layer of the aioli over each toasted bread slice.

5. Spoon the panzanella mixture on top of the sauced toasts. Finish off with a final crank of fresh pepper and eat with a fork and knife, or with your hands.

SERVES 4
1 HOUR

1 large eggplant (about 2 pounds), peeled and cut crosswise into rounds, ½ inch thick

¼ cup extra-virgin olive oil, plus 2 tablespoons

Kosher salt

¼ teaspoon saffron threads (optional)

1 large yellow onion, thinly sliced

4 large garlic cloves, minced

1 tablespoon dried mint, plus more to taste

¼ teaspoon ground turmeric

¼ cup water

¼ cup liquid kashk, plus more to taste and for drizzling (see note)

Warmed sangak, for serving

Liquid kashk is a popular Persian yogurt whey that's pleasantly tangy and sour. It can be found online or at your local Persian market. If your kashk is very thick, thin it by whisking with a tablespoon or two of water until it has the texture of heavy cream. You can substitute with buttermilk (although I highly recommend this recipe with kashk!).

KASHKE BADEMJAN WITH A LOTTA KASHK

Kashke bademjan, also known as Persian eggplant dip, is a creamy, tangy dip that is mixed with kashk, also known as yogurt whey. Kashk adds a sour and tangy contrast and helps cut the richness from the softened eggplant, called bademjan in Farsi. Everything is tossed together with bloomed saffron, mint, and lots of caramelized onions. Here it is served with warmed sangak, a type of bread you can find at most local Persian grocery stores.

1. Preheat your oven to 400°F. Line a large sheet pan with parchment paper.

2. Arrange the eggplant on the lined sheet pan in a single layer and drizzle with ¼ cup of the olive oil. Season both sides with salt. Transfer to the oven and roast until the eggplant has gotten some char and softened, 30 to 40 minutes, flipping halfway through.

3. While your eggplant is roasting, prepare the saffron (if using). Put it in a mortar and pestle and grind into a pasty powder. (If you don't have a mortar and pestle, just grind between your fingers and place in a cup.) Add 2 small ice cubes or 1 tablespoon ice water. Allow the ice to melt completely, which will bloom your saffron.

4. In a large cast-iron skillet or heavy-bottomed pan with a lid, heat your remaining 2 tablespoons olive oil over medium-high heat until shimmering. Add your onions and sauté, stirring often, until they are soft and browned (but not burnt) in places, about 10 minutes.

5. Reduce the heat to low and add your garlic and mint. Sauté until the garlic is fragrant, 1 to 2 minutes. Season with salt to taste. Remove from the heat. Scoop out half of the onion mixture and set aside for topping. Leave the rest in the pan.

6. When your eggplant is ready, transfer (with any oil still on the baking sheet) into the skillet with the onions. Add your turmeric and toss to combine. Increase the heat to medium-low, add the water, cover and steam until your eggplant is completely soft, about 5 minutes.

7. Remove from the heat and mash until mostly smooth with some chunks. You can use a mortar and pestle here, a fork, or a potato masher. Add the bloomed saffron (if using), liquid kashk, and salt to taste. Mix well.

8. Pour the dip in a shallow serving bowl and top with your reserved caramelized onions. Drizzle with more kashk to taste. Serve warm, with sangak.

SERVES 2
30 MINUTES

SHAKSHUKA RANCHEROS WITH ZESTY CREMA

I grew up eating shakshuka, a Tunisian and West African egg staple, also popular in Middle Eastern cooking. Eggs stewed in a rich, tomato-filled base is my comfort food and one of my favorite meals. Another favorite is huevos rancheros, a popular classic Mexican egg dish, where the tomatoes and eggs are placed on top of crispy tortillas. So, I knew combining the two would be a match made in heaven! Serve with a zesty crema, which adds a nice cooling finish to these rancheros.

SHAKSHUKA RANCHEROS

3 tablespoons neutral oil

4 corn tortillas

1 small yellow onion, finely chopped

2 small garlic cloves, minced

1 teaspoon harissa paste

1 teaspoon ground cumin

Kosher salt and freshly ground black pepper

One 14.5-ounce can crushed fire-roasted tomatoes

½ cup water

4 large eggs

ZESTY CREMA

¼ cup sour cream

Grated zest and juice of ½ large lime, plus remaining ½ for serving

Kosher salt and freshly ground black pepper

Finely chopped fresh cilantro, for serving

1. **Make your Shakshuka Rancheros:** Line a plate with paper towels and have it near the stove. In a large shallow pot or large skillet with a lid, heat 1 tablespoon of the oil over medium heat. Add your corn tortillas and lightly fry them, flipping periodically, until they have a nice crunch with a subtle light brown color, 5 to 7 minutes. You don't want them too crisp, or too soft. Do this in batches as needed and transfer to the paper towels to drain any excess oil.

2. Add the remaining 2 tablespoons oil and the onion to the pan and sauté until translucent, 3 to 4 minutes. Add your garlic, harissa paste, cumin, and salt and pepper to taste. Stir until combined and cook until your onions and garlic are soft, another 1 to 2 minutes.

3. Pour in your crushed tomatoes, and then pour the water into the tomato can and swirl to get out any remaining tomato sauce, adding it to the skillet. Toss to combine, reduce the heat to low, and simmer until the mixture has thickened and darkened slightly, 5 to 6 minutes. The consistency should be similar to that of marinara sauce. Season with salt and pepper.

4. Make 4 wells in your tomato mixture with a spoon and gently crack an egg into each well. Cover the pan, increase the heat to medium-low, and simmer gently until the whites are set and the yolks are runny, 3 to 4 minutes.

5. **Make your Zesty Crema:** While your eggs are cooking, in a small bowl, stir together the sour cream, lime zest, lime juice, and salt and pepper to taste.

6. **To serve:** Set 2 corn tortillas on each of two plates. Top each with 2 eggs and spoon the tomato sauce over them. Top with a dollop of crema, a crank of pepper, and chopped cilantro. Finish with a squeeze of lime juice. Eat with a fork and knife.

SERVES 6
15 MINUTES

ANCHOVY & PEPPERONCINI OLIVE TAPENADE CROSTINI

1 cup pitted Kalamata olives, drained

1 cup pitted Castelvetrano olives, drained

¼ cup sliced pepperoncini peppers or 3 whole pepperoncini peppers, stems removed, and 1 tablespoon pepperoncini juice, plus more to taste

¼ cup roughly torn fresh flat-leaf parsley

3 to 4 anchovy fillets, plus more (optional) for serving

2 small garlic cloves, peeled but whole

¼ cup extra-virgin olive oil

Kosher salt and freshly ground black pepper

¼-inch slices baguette, toasted

Vegan/vegetarian option: Omit the anchovy fillets.

This tapenade will be just as delicious served with some crudités, alongside Roasted Garlic Tarragon Yogurt Dip (page 28).

Anchovies can transform a dish in the most surprising way. Most of the time, you can't even tell when they have been added, yet they still give an umami punch. I remember being shocked to find out that Caesar dressing, my favorite, is made with anchovies! While I was late to the anchovy party, it has become a staple in my pantry, and I find myself adding it to a variety of dishes. The nutty, salty flavor adds zest and all-around savoriness. Olives and pepperoncini are the perfect accompaniment to the anchovies. I like to save whole anchovy fillets to serve directly on top of the tapenade crostini.

1. **Equipment:** Bring out your food processor.

2. **Make your tapenade:** In the food processor, combine the pitted olives, pepperoncini peppers, pepperoncini juice, parsley, anchovy fillets, and garlic. Pulse the mixture until everything is finely chopped and combined, 1 to 2 minutes. (You can also chop this all finely by hand, if you prefer.)

3. With the food processor running or pulsing, slowly drizzle in the olive oil until the tapenade comes together, 1 to 2 minutes. You can leave it slightly chunky or process it until smooth. I prefer it somewhere in-between, not too smooth, but also not too chunky.

4. Taste and season with pepperoncini juice, salt, and black pepper, if needed, and give it one more pulse to combine. The anchovies and olives are already salty, so you may not need any additional salt!

5. **To assmble:** Spoon a generous amount of the tapenade onto each toasted baguette slice. If you'd like, garnish each crostini with a whole anchovy fillet.

SERVES 4
30 MINUTES

VERY SHALLOT-Y MAYO

¼ cup mayonnaise

2 tablespoons minced shallot (about 1 small)

½ teaspoon distilled white vinegar

Kosher salt and freshly ground black pepper

MLTS

Kosher salt

2 medium heirloom tomatoes, cut into slices ½ inch thick

16 slices mortadella, folded in quarters

8 slices sourdough bread

2 small heads butter lettuce

MLT WITH VERY SHALLOT-Y MAYO

A BLT is always a popular option, but have you ever tried an MLT, a mortadella, lettuce, and tomato sandwich? If you're looking to switch things up, exchanging bacon for mortadella is the way to go.

We begin by salting the tomatoes, which helps bring out the sweetness and also helps release moisture. This ensures we're not having a soggy sandwich (no one wants that). Pan-frying mortadella crisps it in no time, and you can save time and capture flavor by using the same pan to toast the bread. This sandwich is balanced out with a very pungent shallot mayo that adds even more crunch, creaminess, and texture.

1. **Make your Very Shallot-y Mayo:** In a small bowl, mix together the mayonnaise, shallots, vinegar, and salt and black pepper to taste.

2. **Make your MLTs:** Salt your sliced tomatoes and set aside for about 10 minutes.

3. Meanwhile, line a plate with paper towels and set near the stove. Heat a large skillet over medium-high heat. Working in batches, add your folded mortadella and fry for 2 to 3 minutes on each side. It should get a nice sear and char, and crust up a bit! Once seared, transfer to the paper towels.

4. If you want to toast the bread, use the same skillet and toast the slices over medium-high heat. Do this in batches if needed. If not toasting, then skip this step.

5. **To assemble your sandwiches:** Spread the mayo on half of the bread slices (or on all of the bread slices, which is what I like to do, but it's up to you). Top with 4 or 5 leaves of butter lettuce, followed by tomatoes and your crispy mortadella. Close the sandwiches, cut in half, and serve.

SERVES 4
30 MINUTES

ROSEMARY BUTTER BEANS WITH HEAVY PEPPER & PECORINO

2 tablespoons extra-virgin olive oil, plus more for drizzling

8 small garlic cloves, thinly sliced

2 teaspoons freshly ground black pepper, plus more for serving

Kosher salt

Two 15- to 15.5-ounce cans butter beans, undrained

Two 3-inch sprigs fresh rosemary

4 tablespoons unsalted butter, cubed and cold

¼ cup grated Pecorino Romano cheese, plus more shaved slices for serving

½ cup water

2 teaspoons sherry vinegar

Crusty bread, for serving

Pecorino Romano cheese is quite salty, so keep in mind when adding salt to taste!

Inspired by the classic Italian *cacio e pepe*, meaning "cheese and pepper," these butter beans go heavy on the pepper and creaminess from the salty Pecorino Romano. Butter beans, also called lima beans, are bigger beans than most, so when you simmer them in this creamy sauce, the flesh on the inside of the beans becomes extremely tender. Soak up all the saucy goodness with some crusty bread for the most satisfying bite you can make in under 30 minutes.

1. In a large skillet or pot, heat the olive oil over medium heat. Add the garlic and black pepper. Season with salt. Sauté for 2 to 3 minutes, being careful not to burn the garlic. This will help infuse the oil with all those lovely garlic flavors and bloom your pepper!

2. Add your butter beans, including the canning liquid, and the rosemary sprigs. Increase the heat to medium-high and cook until the beans are hot and some of the canning liquid has reduced, stirring occasionally, about 5 minutes.

3. Reduce the heat to medium and add the butter to the skillet. Allow the butter to melt into the beans for another couple of minutes, then mix well to combine. Turn off the heat.

4. Discard the rosemary sprigs. Stir in the grated Pecorino Romano cheese until it's fully melted and incorporated into the beans. Finish with the water and the sherry vinegar, tossing to combine. The beans should be creamy, but also a little glossy and saucy.

5. Transfer your beans to shallow plates or bowls. Finish with an extra drizzle of olive oil and a healthy crank of black pepper, then use a vegetable peeler to shave some Pecorino Romano cheese over the top. Serve with crusty bread.

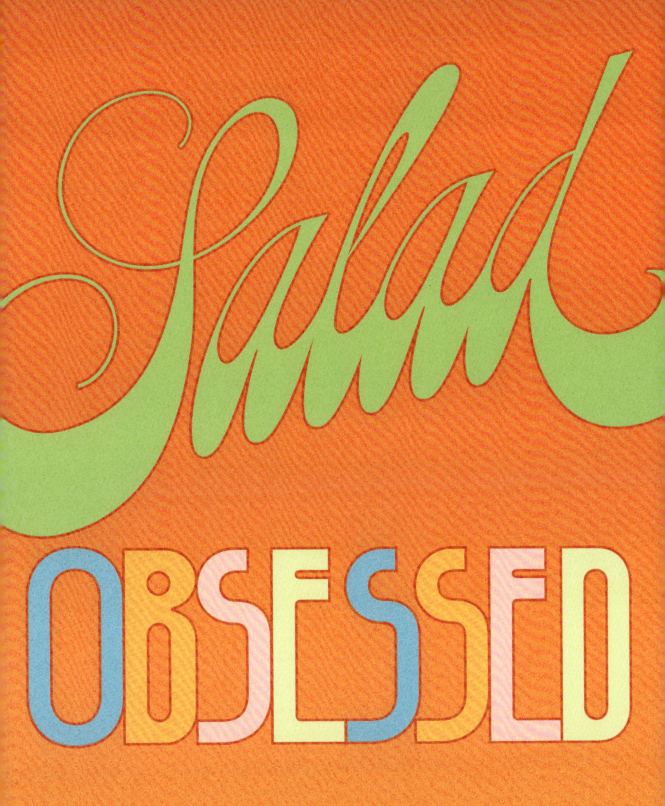

SERVES 4
1 HOUR

KINDA NIÇOISE WITH FARRO & SMASHED CAPER DRESSING

1 cup farro

4 large eggs

Kosher salt

1 pound green beans, trimmed and sliced crosswise into ½-inch pieces

SMASHED CAPER DRESSING

2 tablespoons capers, plus 1 tablespoon caper brine

1 tablespoon sherry vinegar, plus more to taste

1 teaspoon Dijon mustard

¼ cup extra-virgin olive oil

Kosher salt and freshly ground black pepper

SALAD

2 Persian cucumbers, finely diced

1 pint cherry tomatoes, halved

½ small red onion, minced

½ cup finely chopped fresh flat-leaf parsley

½ cup finely chopped fresh dill

Kosher salt and freshly ground black pepper

Make this vegan by taking out the eggs.

Cooked proteins like shrimp, tuna, or chicken (shred chicken from Really Good Roast Chicken, page 155) are great additions.

Niçoise, a popular salad from Nice, is made with hard-boiled eggs, olives, fish, and tomatoes, but there are a number of ways to make this dish. Similar in style to a chopped salad, this "kinda" Niçoise uses a variety of veggies, including the usual suspects as well as farro, all tossed with a briny, tangy caper dressing.

1. Bring a large pot of water to a boil over medium-high heat.

2. Meanwhile, set the farro in a large fine-mesh sieve and rinse under cold water to get rid of any dusty and waxy debris.

3. When the water is boiling, gently lower in your eggs. Cook for 9 minutes, then immediately remove from the water with a spider strainer or fine-mesh sieve, rinse under cold water and set aside to cool. Keep the water boiling.

4. Add the farro and a generous pinch of salt to the boiling water and keep your sieve handy. Cook over medium-high heat until tender with a slight bite to it, checking the texture after 15 minutes. If needed, continue cooking for another 5 to 10 minutes. In the last 3 minutes of boiling, add the green beans. Drain in the sieve you set aside, rinse under cold water, and shake dry.

5. **Make your Smashed Caper Dressing:** While your farro is cooking, in a large bowl, smash the capers with the back of a fork until they are crushed into a rough paste, leaving some chunks for texture. Add the caper brine, vinegar, and mustard. Slowly start whisking in your olive oil until the dressing is creamy and emulsified. Season with salt and black pepper.

6. **Assemble the salad:** In the large bowl with the dressing, stir together the cucumbers, tomatoes, and onion. Add your cooled farro and green beans and toss in the parsley and dill. Season to taste with salt, pepper, and sherry vinegar. I like this extra tangy, so I tend to add an additional tablespoon of vinegar.

7. This can be served immediately, or stored covered in the fridge for up to 4 days! The longer it sits in the fridge, the better.

8. **To serve:** Divide the grain salad among bowls. Peel the eggs and quarter them lengthwise. Top each serving of salad with hard-boiled eggs and a crank of black pepper.

SOMETHING DELICIOUS

SERVES 4
30 MINUTES

LITTLE GEM CAESAR SALAD WITH HABANERO DRESSING & SOURDOUGH BREAD CRUMBS

SOURDOUGH BREAD CRUMBS

2 slices sourdough bread, roughly torn

2 tablespoons extra-virgin olive oil

Kosher salt and freshly ground black pepper

HABANERO DRESSING

3 to 4 oil-packed anchovy fillets

2 large garlic cloves, peeled but whole

2 egg yolks

1 teaspoon Dijon mustard

1 habanero, seeded (½ if you want this less spicy)

1 teaspoon Worcestershire sauce

Juice of 1 small lemon

Kosher salt and freshly ground black pepper

¼ cup extra-virgin olive oil

¼ cup neutral oil

¼ cup shredded Parmigiano-Reggiano cheese

LITTLE GEM CAESAR SALAD

4 heads Little Gem lettuce, leaves pulled apart, washed and dried

Kosher salt and freshly ground black pepper

¼ cup shredded Parmigiano-Reggiano cheese

I wasn't the biggest salad fan growing up (I was actually quite the picky eater!), but the one salad I would always order was a Caesar. Maybe because it was covered in a creamy dressing, loads of Parmesan, and croutons. A favorite Caesar of mine is from Jon & Vinny's in Los Angeles. Theirs is made with little gems, a spicy Calabrian chili dressing and panko bread crumbs instead of croutons. Here, we're layering off their flavors with sourdough bread crumbs and a spicy habanero Caesar dressing (and yes, we're using raw egg yolks and anchovies).

1. **Equipment:** Get out your food processor.

2. **Make your Sourdough Bread Crumbs:** In a food processor, pulse your bread into coarse, mixed-texture crumbs. I will pulse for a few minutes, allowing some crumbs to form, while also keeping some pieces thicker than a panko bread crumb.

3. In a medium skillet, heat the olive oil over medium-high heat until shimmering. Add your bread crumbs to the heated pan (reserve your food processor bowl to make the dressing), and season with salt and black pepper. Stir every few minutes until the bread crumbs have a darkened color, 5 to 7 minutes. Set aside to cool.

4. **Make your Habanero Dressing:** In the food processor, combine the anchovies, garlic, egg yolks, mustard, habanero, Worcestershire sauce, and lemon juice. Season with salt and freshly ground black pepper. Pulse to combine.

5. While continuing to pulse, slowly start streaming in your olive oil. Then stream in your neutral oil, continuing to pulse until everything is emulsified, 3 to 4 minutes. This may look a bit runny, but it will firm up.

6. Transfer the dressing to a large bowl and toss in your shredded Parmesan. Mix to combine. Season with black pepper to taste. Reserve about 1 tablespoon of dressing, for serving.

7. **Assemble the salad:** To the large bowl with the dressing, add your lettuce and season with salt and black pepper. Toss to combine.

8. Transfer your tossed greens to a serving plate or platter. Finish by topping with the shredded cheese, bread crumbs, and a drizzle of your reserved dressing with a big crank of black pepper.

SERVES 4
15 MINUTES

SPICY CRUSHED CUCUMBER SALAD WITH FETA & MINT

4 Persian cucumbers

1 tablespoon freshly squeezed mandarin, tangerine, or orange juice

Kosher salt

10 to 12 fresh mint leaves, torn

¼ cup Sumac & Saffron Chili Crisp (page 32), plus more to taste

¼ cup crumbled feta cheese

Toasted sesame seeds, for serving

Inspired by the traditional Asian cold dish of smashed cucumbers with chili oil, this one is a fusion that combines elements of that refreshing favorite with Persian flavors such as sumac and saffron. By smashing the cucumbers with the side of a knife, you allow the flavors of the chili crisp to seep into all the crevices. A little mandarin orange juice and fresh mint go a long way to balance out both the sumac and saffron in the spicy chili crisp.

1. Quarter the cucumbers lengthwise. With the flesh-side up, use a meat mallet or the flat side of a knife to crush your cucumbers, then cut crosswise into 1-inch pieces.

2. Transfer to a bowl and toss with the mandarin juice and salt to taste. Add the mint leaves and do a final toss with the chili crisp. Transfer to a shallow bowl and top with the crumbled feta and toasted sesame seeds. Serve immediately.

SERVES 4
15 MINUTES

4 medium heads Belgian endive

1 tablespoon whole-grain mustard

Juice of 1 small lemon

Kosher salt and freshly ground black pepper

¼ cup extra-virgin olive oil

ENDIVE & WHOLE-GRAIN MUSTARD SALAD

Endive is a crisp, crunchy, and bitter lettuce from the chicory family. One of my favorite ways to prepare it is with this whole-grain mustard dressing, which helps balance out some of the bitterness from the endive in its raw form. Whole-grain mustard also adds a bit more bite and coarse texture to this salad. Pair this with Crispy Sesame & Herb Chicken Schnitzel (page 173) and you've hit the jackpot for the most perfect dinner.

1. Trim off and discard about 1 inch off the bottoms of your endive. Halve the endives lengthwise at a slight angle, then carefully tear apart the leaves, trimming the end root as you get to the core.

2. In a large bowl, whisk together the mustard, lemon juice, and salt and black pepper to taste. Slowly stream in your olive oil as you continue whisking to emulsify fully.

3. Add the endive and toss to combine.

SERVES 4
30 MINUTES

STEAKHOUSE WEDGE SALAD WITH GORGONZOLA DRESSING & BACON BREAD CRUMBS

BACON BREAD CRUMBS

4 ounces sliced hickory-smoked bacon

¼ cup panko bread crumbs

Kosher salt and freshly ground black pepper

GORGONZOLA DRESSING

¼ cup crumbled Gorgonzola cheese

¼ cup full-fat buttermilk

2 tablespoons mayonnaise

2 tablespoons whole-milk Greek yogurt

1 teaspoon distilled white vinegar, plus more for drizzling

1 teaspoon Worcestershire sauce

2 tablespoons finely chopped fresh chives, plus more for serving

Kosher salt and freshly ground black pepper

STEAKHOUSE WEDGE SALAD

1 medium head iceberg lettuce, cut into quarters

Kosher salt and freshly ground black pepper

½ cup halved cherry tomatoes

Prep your dressing and bread crumbs up to a day ahead and place in the fridge. Bring your bread crumbs to room temperature before serving.

If I'm at a steakhouse and there is a wedge on the menu, I am ordering it! Iceberg lettuce is crunchy and refreshing, and eating it as a wedge with all the fixin's is a truly spiritual experience.

Instead of bacon chunks *and* croutons separately, I'm putting them together here to make crumbled bacony bread crumbs, which are crunchy and smoky. Drizzle the wedge with a Gorgonzola dressing, which is a little more subtle than blue cheese, and top with cherry tomatoes; it's what I would call my dream salad.

1. **Make your Bacon Bread Crumbs:** Line a plate with paper towels and have near the stove. In a medium skillet, arrange the bacon in a single layer. Set the pan over medium heat and let the bacon cook undisturbed for a few minutes until the edges start to curl and turn brown. The bacon will be sizzling and crackling. Using tongs, flip the bacon and cook until crispy, 5 to 7 minutes. Transfer to the paper towels to cool and drain and set aside.

2. Pour off all but 1 tablespoon of bacon fat from the skillet. Add your panko bread crumbs to the skillet and season with salt and black pepper. Reduce the heat to medium-low and cook, stirring occasionally, until golden and toasted, 5 to 7 minutes. Immediately transfer to a small bowl and set aside to cool.

3. Use your fingers to break up the cooled bacon into fine crumbs, then toss with your panko mixture.

4. **Make the Gorgonzola Dressing:** In a small bowl, mash your Gorgonzola as finely as you can, almost into a paste—some chunks are fine. Mix in the buttermilk, mayonnaise, Greek yogurt, vinegar, Worcestershire sauce, and chives. Whisk until well combined, and season with salt and black pepper to taste.

5. **Assemble the salad:** Lay out your iceberg quarters on a platter and season with salt, black pepper, and a drizzle of vinegar between the leaves and sides of the iceberg. Drizzle the dressing generously all over the exterior of the iceberg, in addition to the layers in between. Top with your cherry tomatoes, chives and a good amount of your bacon bread crumbs. I like to give a big crank of black pepper on top of everything. Serve any additional dressing on the side for more drizzling, as needed!

SERVES 4
1 HOUR 15 MINUTES

BEET & PEACH SALAD WITH BURRATA, TOASTED HAZELNUTS & GREEN GODDESS VINAIGRETTE

ROASTED BEETS

1 pound red beets (3 to 4 medium), any stems removed

1 pound yellow beets (3 to 4 medium), any stems removed

Kosher salt

Extra-virgin olive oil, for drizzling

GREEN GODDESS VINAIGRETTE

A large handful of fresh basil leaves, plus leaves for garnish

A large handful of fresh mint leaves

½ cup extra-virgin olive oil

1 to 2 tablespoons sherry vinegar (I like it tangy!)

Kosher salt and freshly ground black pepper

SALAD

½ cup skin-on hazelnuts

Kosher salt

2 yellow peaches, cut into 1-inch wedges

8 ounces burrata cheese

I am not always a fan of fruit in my salad. I make very few exceptions, but this is one of them! I mean, how can you say no to beets and peaches tossed with an herby green goddess vinaigrette? You just can't. With its sweet and earthy flavors, topped with the crunch of toasty hazelnuts and creamy burrata, there is quite literally nothing better than this. While I do suggest roasting your own beets, you can also use store-bought steamed beets.

1. **Equipment:** Bring out your stand blender.

2. **Roast the beets:** Preheat your oven to 400°F.

3. Tear off two large sheets of aluminum foil. Add the red beets to one sheet and the yellow beets to the other. Season with salt and a drizzle of olive oil. Wrap completely, place on a baking dish, and roast until fork-tender, about 1 hour. Remove from the oven, pull open the foil slightly to allow steam to escape, and let cool until just barely warm (or until totally cool).

4. **Make your Green Goddess Vinaigrette:** While your beets are roasting, in the blender, combine the basil, mint, olive oil, vinegar, and salt and black pepper to taste. Blend until completely emulsified and smooth. Transfer to a bowl or bottle.

5. **Toast your hazelnuts:** Place the nuts and a pinch of salt in a dry skillet over medium-low heat. Keep stirring around so they toast evenly on all sides without burning, 7 to 8 minutes. Season to taste with more salt. They should have a toasty aroma. Set aside to cool, then roughly chop.

6. When your beets are cooled, remove from the foil and use your hands to rub off the skins (you can use the foil itself, gloves, or a paper towel here). The skins should come off easily. Cut into 1-inch wedges.

7. **Assemble the salad:** Place your beets in a serving dish along with the peaches, then tear your burrata over the dish, scattering it evenly. Drizzle with half the vinaigrette (pass the rest at the table!), sprinkle with the toasted hazelnuts, and garnish with fresh basil leaves.

SERVES 4
15 MINUTES

BUTTER LETTUCE & AVOCADO SALAD WITH UNCLE IRA'S "GOOD DRESSING"

In our family, we call this Uncle Ira's "Good Dressing," and it is definitely a hot commodity. At every single family gathering you can count on someone asking, "Is this Uncle Ira's 'Good Dressing?'" While we serve it in the biggest gravy boat we can find, there still never seems to be enough! Its tangy flavors from the shallots, balsamic vinegar, and Dijon mustard liven up any salad. Here we're tossing it with crisp butter lettuce and avocado, but you can mix and match with any of your favorite vegetables and greens.

UNCLE IRA'S "GOOD DRESSING"

1 small shallot, minced

¼ cup balsamic vinegar

1 tablespoon Dijon mustard

Kosher salt and freshly ground black pepper

½ cup extra-virgin olive oil

BUTTER LETTUCE & AVOCADO SALAD

2 heads green or red butter lettuce, leaves separated (tear any large ones), washed and dried

1 avocado, sliced

Freshly ground black pepper

1. **Prepare Uncle Ira's "Good Dressing":** In a medium bowl, combine your shallot, vinegar, mustard, salt, and black pepper to taste. Mix well until combined. Slowly stream in your olive oil, whisking constantly until emulsified, creamy, and dark brown. Cover and transfer to the fridge until ready to serve. (If making ahead, combine all the ingredients in a screw-top jar or deli container and shake well until emulsified. Store in the fridge for up to 3 days.)

2. **Assemble your salad:** In a large salad bowl, combine the butter lettuce and your desired amount of dressing and give it a light toss to combine.

3. Transfer to a serving platter and gently nestle in your avocado slices, finishing with a crank of black pepper. Serve with more dressing alongside the salad if anyone wants to drizzle more (they *will* want to!).

SERVES 4
15 MINUTES

RADICCHIO & FENNEL SALAD WITH ORANGE MAPLE POPPY SEED VINAIGRETTE

ORANGE MAPLE POPPY SEED VINAIGRETTE

¼ cup freshly squeezed orange juice (about 1 medium orange)

1 tablespoon maple syrup

2 teaspoons Dijon mustard

2 teaspoons poppy seeds

1½ teaspoons sherry vinegar

Kosher salt and freshly ground black pepper

¼ cup extra-virgin olive oil

RADICCHIO & FENNEL SALAD

1 large fennel bulb, with fronds

1 small Treviso radicchio, halved and thinly sliced crosswise

1 small Castelfranco radicchio, halved and thinly sliced crosswise

½ cup finely chopped fresh flat-leaf parsley

Freshly ground black pepper

¼ cup shaved Parmigiano-Reggiano cheese

Vegan/dairy-free option: Omit the shaved Parmesan.

Radicchio, a member of the chicory family, has a bitter, punchy flavor and adds a splash of color to any salad. Here the bitterness from the radicchio is balanced out by the sweet and tangy maple vinaigrette, with a crisp texture from the poppy seeds. The thinly sliced fennel gives this a hint of licorice flavor (don't worry, it's not what you think), as well as an incredible bit of crunch and tang. Endives or Chioggia radicchio will work great as substitutions if you can't get your hands on Treviso or Castelfranco.

Sometimes I like to make this vinaigrette separately in a deli container or mason jar to prep ahead and keep in the fridge. Just pour all the dressing ingredients together and shake really well until emulsified!

1. **Make your Orange Maple Poppy Seed Vinaigrette:** In a large bowl, whisk together the orange juice, maple syrup, mustard, poppy seeds, vinegar, and salt and black pepper to taste. Whisking constantly, slowly start streaming in your olive oil until the dressing is creamy and emulsified.

2. **Prep your fennel:** Cut off the fronds from your fennel bulb, tear into small pieces, and set aside, discarding the stalks. Cut off the butt of the hard core of your fennel, then cut in half lengthwise, removing any tough outer layers. Then thinly slice lengthwise.

3. To the bowl with the dressing, add your fennel, Treviso and Castelfranco radicchio, a few tablespoons of chopped fennel fronds, and the parsley. Toss to combine all your vegetables and the dressing together, until evenly coated.

4. **To serve:** Pile in a shallow bowl (or keep it in the large bowl it was mixed in) and top with a big crank of black pepper. Top with a good amount of shaved Parmesan cheese.

SERVES 4
15 MINUTES

CUCUMBER, CANTALOUPE & TOMATO SALAD WITH RANCH-ISH DRESSING

RANCH-ISH DRESSING

¼ cup full-fat buttermilk

⅓ cup mayonnaise

¼ cup chopped fresh chives

1 small garlic clove, grated

Grated zest and juice of ½ small lemon, plus more to taste

Kosher salt and freshly ground black pepper

CUCUMBER, CANTALOUPE & TOMATO SALAD

1 small cantaloupe (about 2 pounds), peeled and cut into bite-size cubes

9 medium tomatoes (about 1 pound), quartered

2 Persian cucumbers, halved lengthwise and cut crosswise into ½-inch half-moons

¼ cup finely chopped fresh chives, plus more for serving

Kosher salt and freshly ground black pepper

Sweet, tangy, and refreshing, this salad is served with a ranch-style dressing and is perfect when the sun is shining. Cucumbers, cantaloupe, and vine-ripened red tomatoes are tossed with fresh chives. This almost gives diner vibes, sort of like a saucy wedge salad. I love Early Girl tomatoes in the summertime for this recipe, but you can use any tomatoes you have on hand, such as Roma, cherry tomatoes, or heirloom.

1. **Make your Ranch-Ish Dressing:** In a small bowl, whisk together the buttermilk, mayonnaise, chives, garlic, lemon zest, lemon juice, and salt and black pepper to taste.

2. **Prepare your salad:** In a large serving bowl, toss together your cantaloupe, tomatoes, cucumbers, and chives. Season with salt and pepper, tossing to coat.

3. Drizzle over half of the dressing. Garnish with the additional chopped chives and black pepper. Serve the remaining dressing on the side for even more drizzling. You can also store this salad in the fridge for up to 4 to 5 hours until ready to eat.

Cozy Stews,

Soups, & Broths

SERVES 4
30 MINUTES

TURMERIC DAL WITH MINTY-LIME YOGURT & CRISPY ONIONS

TURMERIC DAL

2 tablespoons unsalted butter, ghee, or neutral oil

½ cup finely chopped yellow onion

2 large garlic cloves, minced or grated

1-inch piece fresh ginger, peeled and minced or grated

1 teaspoon curry powder (or ½ teaspoon ground cumin and ½ teaspoon ground coriander)

½ teaspoon garam masala

½ teaspoon ground turmeric

¼ teaspoon chili powder, red pepper flakes, or cayenne pepper

Kosher salt and freshly ground black pepper

1½ cups red lentils, rinsed

4 cups water, or more as needed

CRISPY ONIONS

¼ cup neutral oil

1 large yellow onion, thinly sliced

Kosher salt

MINTY-LIME YOGURT

1 cup whole-milk Greek yogurt

Juice of 1 large lime, plus lime wedges for squeezing

¼ cup finely chopped fresh mint, plus more for serving

Kosher salt and freshly ground black pepper

A Pot o' Rice (page 228)

Chili Crisp (page 32), optional

Dal is something I grew up eating, lovingly prepared by all my aunts (Mom not included). If you've never had dal before, it is a classic Indian stew of spices and lentils. Each one of my aunts has her own unique way of making this comfort dish. My Aunt Lulu adds amchoor (dried mango powder), Aunt Nina adds fresh cilantro and jalapeño, Aunt Renee makes a tadka (a sizzled chili spiced oil, or ghee, which is spooned over top), and Aunt Florette blends most of the mixture for a smooth finish. However, there is one thing they all have in common: They are all something delicious!

My take: Adding mint yogurt and crispy onions, I'm taking inspiration from the Persian soup ash, Danny's favorite. The crunch from the onions works so well with the cooling effect from the yogurt and dal.

1. **Make your Turmeric Dal:** In a large saucepan or Dutch oven with a lid, heat the butter over medium heat until glistening. Add the onion and sauté until translucent, 1 to 2 minutes. Add your garlic and ginger, tossing to combine. Add the curry powder, garam masala, turmeric, chili powder, and salt and black pepper, stirring constantly, until the spices are fragrant but not browned, 1 to 2 minutes or until fragrant.

2. Toss in your rinsed lentils and do a final stir. Add the water and bring to a boil. Reduce the heat to medium-low, cover, and simmer, stirring occasionally, until the lentils are tender and the dal has thickened significantly, 15 to 20 minutes. If you find it is getting too thick for your preference, adjust with a dash of water, as needed, tossing to combine.

3. **Make your Crispy Onions:** While your lentils are cooking, line a plate with paper towels and set near the stove. In a small deep pan, combine the neutral oil and onions and bring the heat to medium-high. Stir frequently, until the onions become golden brown and crisp, 10 to 15 minutes. Transfer to the paper towels to drain any excess oil. Season with salt. Store any oil from the pan in a mason jar or squeeze bottle for up to a week for use in any future cooking (such as eggs or salad dressings!).

4. **Make your Minty-Lime Yogurt:** In a medium bowl, combine the yogurt, lime juice, mint, and salt and pepper to taste. Mix well, cover, and refrigerate until ready to serve.

5. **To serve:** Ladle your dal into serving bowls over rice, topping with a dollop of minty-lime yogurt, crispy onions, mint, lime juice, and Chili Crisp (if using).

SERVES 4
45 MINUTES

2 large bunches of broccolini (about 2 pounds total)

¼ cup extra-virgin olive oil, plus more for drizzling

1 large shallot, minced

Kosher salt and freshly ground black pepper

2 large garlic cloves, minced

4 cups vegetable broth

¼ cup heavy cream, plus more for drizzling

4 ounces smoked Gouda cheese

1 teaspoon sherry vinegar, plus more to taste

CREAM OF BROCCOLINI & SMOKED GOUDA SOUP

I love the sharpness from Cheddar cheese blended with earthy broccoli in broccoli-Cheddar soup—it is just perfect. But let's give it an upgrade with broccolini, a more subtle sweet veg, and smoked Gouda. Not only will you get the familiar sharpness, but you'll also get a really deep, smoky flavor from the Gouda! If you're not into the smoky flavor, you can use regular Gouda here instead.

1. **Equipment:** Bring out your stand blender or immersion blender.

2. Cut ½ inch off the bottom of your broccolini stems and discard any tough bottom bits. Then thinly slice the stems. Slice the leaves lengthwise, chopping them into even pieces, and keeping the florets whole.

3. In a medium pot, heat up your olive oil over medium-high heat until glistening. Add your shallots and stir occasionally for a minute. Season with salt and pepper. Add your garlic cloves and give everything a nice toss until your garlic has softened, 1 to 2 minutes.

4. Add your broccolini, season with salt and pepper, and let everything combine together until your broccolini turns a nice vibrant green, 2 to 3 minutes.

5. Add your broth and bring to a boil. Reduce the heat to medium-low and simmer until your broccolini is soft and fork tender, 10 to 15 minutes. While your broccolini is cooking, grate your Gouda; you should have about 1 cup shredded.

6. With an immersion blender or stand blender, blend the soup until completely smooth and creamy, with no clumps. If using a stand blender, make sure to open the steam vent in the lid. Return the soup to the pot.

7. Set the pot over low heat and stir in your heavy cream. Slowly start adding your Gouda, stirring to combine and melt throughout. Turn off the heat and finish by tossing in the vinegar. Season to taste with salt, pepper, and vinegar.

8. Serve in bowls and top with a drizzle of olive oil, a drizzle of cream, and freshly ground black pepper.

SERVES 4
1 HOUR

BEET SOUP WITH FENNEL, ONIONS & HORSERADISH CREAM

This beet soup is inspired by a classic borscht from Eastern Europe. Traditionally made with a variety of vegetables—and beef—borscht always has beets at the center of the dish. This version is made with red beets and potatoes, a zingy horseradish cream, and a fennel and onion salad on top. With its deep pink color from the beets and the crunch of the fennel and onions, you have one beautiful and tasty combo.

BEET SOUP

1 teaspoon fennel seeds

1 tablespoon extra-virgin olive oil

Kosher salt and freshly ground black pepper

½ large yellow onion, minced

2 tablespoons tomato paste

5 medium red beets (about 1½ pounds), peeled and cut into ½-inch cubes

3 medium Yukon Gold potatoes (about 1½ pounds), cut into ½-inch bite-size pieces

4 cups vegetable broth

FENNEL & ONION SALAD

1 large fennel bulb

½ yellow onion, thinly sliced

¼ cup roughly chopped fresh dill

Juice of ½ small lemon

Kosher salt and freshly ground black pepper

HORSERADISH CREAM

½ cup sour cream

1 teaspoon prepared horseradish, plus more to taste

Juice of ½ small lemon

Kosher salt and freshly ground black pepper

TO FINISH

1 teaspoon granulated sugar

Toasted rye bread, for serving

Vegan/dairy-free option: Omit the horseradish cream!

1. **Make your Beet Soup:** In a mortar and pestle, grind your fennel seeds until you get a coarse powder. Set a large Dutch oven or pot over medium heat and drizzle in the olive oil. Add your fennel seeds and salt and pepper to bloom for 1 minute until fragrant, stirring to evenly distribute the oil over the spices.

2. Add your onion and tomato paste and stir until the tomato paste turns a dark auburn and the onions are softened, 3 to 4 minutes.

3. Add your beets and potatoes, tossing to combine. Season with salt and pepper. Add your broth and bring to a boil over medium-high heat. Reduce the heat to medium-low and simmer uncovered, until your beets and potatoes are fork-tender, 40 to 45 minutes.

4. **Make your Fennel & Onion Salad:** While the vegetables are simmering, tear the fennel fronds into small pieces and set aside about 2 tablespoons to use in the recipe; reserve the rest for another use. To prepare the bulb, trim off the stalks; they can be used for stock or discarded. Cut off the butt of the hard core of your fennel, then cut in half lengthwise, removing any tough outer layers. Then thinly slice lengthwise.

5. In a large bowl, toss together the sliced fennel, fennel fronds, onion, dill, lemon juice, and salt and pepper to taste.

6. **Mix your Horseradish Cream:** In a medium bowl, stir together the sour cream, horseradish, lemon juice, and salt and pepper to taste. Adjust with more horseradish to taste.

7. To finish your soup, stir in the sugar and adjust with salt and pepper to taste.

8. **To serve:** Ladle the beet soup into bowls. Top with a dollop of the horseradish cream and finish with your fennel and onion salad. Serve with toasted rye bread.

SERVES 4 TO 6
1 HOUR 30 MINUTES

GRANDMA DAISY'S TOMATO & CHICKEN RICE SOUP

TOMATO & CHICKEN RICE SOUP

½ chicken (1½ to 2 pounds), cut into breast, wing, thigh, and drumstick

Kosher salt and freshly ground black pepper

2 tablespoons neutral oil

1 yellow onion, finely chopped

½ teaspoon paprika

⅛ teaspoon ground turmeric

3 large garlic cloves, thinly sliced

¼ cup tomato paste

5 medium Roma tomatoes (1½ pounds), cut into ½-inch cubes (see note)

1 cup long-grain white rice, such as jasmine or basmati, rinsed

6 cups chicken broth, or 4 cups broth plus 2 cups water, plus more as needed

SCALLION SERRANO TOPPING

¼ cup thinly sliced scallions

1 serrano chile, seeded and finely chopped

2 teaspoons fresh lemon juice, plus more for serving

continued...

Whenever I would walk into my grandparents' house growing up, I would get a whiff of this delicious chicken rice soup. My Grandma Daisy would always make a version of this Baghdadi Jewish, Indian-Iraqi soup, and it continues to be a part of our dinner table to this day. It's called *shorba*, and like many tomato chicken rice soups, it begins with a slow-braised chicken in tomatoes and rice, with the addition of ginger and turmeric. The chicken fat gives it a robust flavor, and the tender, fall-off-the-bone meat makes it a meal you will want to have over and over again.

My mom would always eat this with the hottest green chiles she could find, oftentimes panting and tearing up from the heat, as she continued to bite into each pepper one shout at a time. While I never understood why she would put herself through this chile torture, I was inspired to create this serrano scallion topper that is spicy (not as spicy as she'd like), tangy, and definitely brightens up this meal.

Early fall, when it gets chilly and you can find some end-of-season super-duper lovely ripe tomatoes, is the best time to enjoy this.

1. **Make your Tomato & Chicken Rice Soup:** Pat your chicken dry and season on all sides with salt and pepper. In a large Dutch oven or wide pot, heat the neutral oil over high heat. Add your chicken pieces to the pan, skin-side down, and cook and brown the skin, 4 to 5 minutes per side. Transfer to a plate—we will finish cooking the chicken later.

2. Reduce the heat to medium-low, leaving any excess oil and the chicken fat in the pan. Add your onion, paprika, turmeric, and salt and pepper and give the onions a nice toss. Add your garlic and tomato paste and stir until the paste darkens a tad, 2 to 3 minutes.

3. Increase the heat to medium-high. Add your tomatoes, stirring and mashing them to release their juices to form a nice combined sauce with the rest of the pot. This should take 7 to 10 minutes, and it's okay if the tomatoes are a little chunky here, too, but you definitely want to release their juices and form a sauce.

GRANDMA DAISY'S TOMATO & CHICKEN RICE SOUP
continued

If it's not tomato season, put your tomatoes in a bowl with a sprinkle of salt. This brings out their moisture and flavor. Drain and discard the tomato water when ready to use. Proceed with using your tomatoes. If it IS tomato season, you can also use other tomato varieties, such as heirloom, which will be really nice and juicy for this soup!

4. Add the rinsed rice and toss to combine. Nestle in the chicken and pour in your broth. Bring this mixture to a boil. Reduce the heat to a simmer, cover, and cook until your chicken is completely cooked, 30 to 40 minutes. At this point, your mixture should not be too liquidy, and not too thick either. You can adjust with more water or broth as needed here to reach your desired texture.

5. **Make your Scallion Serrano Topping:** While the chicken cooks, in a small bowl, toss together the scallions, serrano, lemon juice, and salt and pepper to taste. Set aside until ready to serve.

6. Carefully transfer your chicken to a bowl and cool until you can handle. Tear the meat off with your hands, or a fork, discarding the bones and skin. I usually don't go too shredded, but just tear it into bite-size pieces.

7. Return the chicken to the soup. Season to taste with salt and pepper, tossing your chicken in the soup. Adjust with more water or broth as preferred.

8. **To serve:** Ladle into bowls, topping with your serrano mixture layered on top. Finish with freshly ground black pepper and a squeeze of lemon juice.

SERVES 4
45 MINUTES

CREAMY TORTILLA SOUP WITH CHILI-LIME STRIPS

CHILI-LIME STRIPS

Two 5- to 6-inch corn tortillas, cut into ½-inch strips

2 tablespoons neutral oil, plus more as needed

½ teaspoon chili powder

Grated zest of ½ large lime, plus lime wedges for squeezing

Kosher salt

CREAMY TORTILLA SOUP

1 large yellow onion, roughly chopped

1 large red bell pepper, roughly chopped

4 large garlic cloves, roughly chopped

2 teaspoons chili powder

Kosher salt and freshly ground black pepper

One 14.5-ounce can diced fire-roasted tomatoes

2 cups vegetable broth, plus more as needed

Two 5- to 6-inch corn tortillas, roughly torn

FOR SERVING

Avocado slices

Fresh cilantro, chopped

Red onion, thinly sliced

While this is dairy-free, if you want to top with some Zesty Crema (page 59), or queso fresco, I won't be mad either.

Creamy but without any cream, this soup has corn tortillas blended right into the broth, giving it a smooth and silky finish. You get all the elements of a traditional tortilla soup with the chili powder and fire-roasted tomatoes all blended together and topped with crispy chili-lime tortilla strips. Add all the toppings your heart desires, like avocado, fresh cilantro, and crunchy sliced red onions.

1. **Equipment:** Bring out your stand blender or immersion blender.

2. **Make your Chili-Lime Strips:** Line a plate with paper towels and have near the stove. In a large pot or Dutch oven, heat your oil over medium-high heat until shimmering and hot. Add your strips to fry, using tongs to separate any that may have clung together. Watch carefully, flipping occasionally until they are crispy and light brown in color, 3 to 5 minutes. Transfer to the paper towels, season immediately with the chili powder, lime zest, and salt to taste.

3. **Make your Creamy Tortilla Soup:** In the same pot you used to make the chili strips, combine the onions and bell pepper, set the pot over medium heat, and sauté until the onions are translucent, 3 to 5 minutes. Adjust with more oil here, if needed.

4. Add your garlic, chili powder, and salt and black pepper to taste. Toss and cook until the bell pepper begins to soften, 2 to 3 minutes longer.

5. Reduce the heat to medium-low, add your fire-roasted tomatoes, and give everything a nice stir. Let the tomatoes cook a tad, until the liquid has reduced by half, 1 to 2 minutes.

6. Add your vegetable broth and torn tortillas (this helps thicken up the soup!) Season with salt and black pepper. Allow everything to simmer at medium-low heat uncovered until all your vegetables and corn tortillas are soft and the flavors are combined, 10 to 12 minutes.

7. Use an immersion blender to blend until completely smooth. (Alternatively, blend in a stand blender, making sure to open up the steam vent. Return the soup to the pot.) Season the soup with salt and thin with additional vegetable broth to desired consistency.

8. **To serve:** Ladle your soup into bowls, top with the chili strips, avocado, cilantro, red onion, and a lime squeeze.

SERVES 4 TO 6
3 HOURS

WHITE MISO & SCALLION BROTHY BEANS

2 tablespoons extra-virgin olive oil, plus more for drizzling

6 large garlic cloves, peeled but whole

4 large shallots, peeled and halved

Two 2-inch thumbs fresh ginger, peeled and cut into thin matchsticks

Kosher salt and freshly ground black pepper

1 pound dried white beans (2¼ cups), such as cannellini or navy beans

8 cups water, plus more as needed

½ cup finely chopped scallions, plus more for serving

2 tablespoons white miso

Brothy beans are one of my favorite cozy, set-it-and-forget-it meals to make. This variation is a play on miso soup, with scallions and miso paste steeped into the flavor-filled broth. It's very ginger-forward too, giving a zing and spice that I love.

These beans are even better the next day and can be stored in the fridge for up to 5 days. If you find that it's too thick the next day, add water when warming.

1. In a large heavy-bottomed pot or Dutch oven, heat the olive oil over medium-high heat. Add your garlic, shallots, and ginger and cook, flipping periodically, until charred on all sides, 8 to 10 minutes. Season with salt and pepper.

2. Add your beans to the pot and pour in the water, adding more as needed to ensure the beans are fully submerged. Bring the mixture to a boil over high heat. Reduce the heat to low, cover, and simmer gently until the beans are completely tender and cooked through, 2 to 3 hours. Stir occasionally and check for seasoning, adding more salt and pepper as needed. (Just keep in mind that you'll be adding some salty miso at the end, too.) If you find that you need more water, feel free to add a cup or two as needed. If you find that your beans need more time, keep them going until they are tender.

3. Just before serving, bring the heat to low. Add the scallions and toss to combine. Ladle a bit of hot bean broth into a small bowl, add the miso, and mix with a fork or whisk until smooth. Pour into the bean pot and stir gently to combine.

4. Ladle into bowls and top with more chopped scallions, a crank more pepper, and a finishing drizzle of olive oil.

SERVES 4
1 HOUR 15 MINUTES

ONE-POT FRENCH ONION & SHALLOT SOUP WITH SOURDOUGH TOASTS

2 tablespoons unsalted butter

1 pound sweet onions (2 to 3 large), such as Vidalia or Walla Walla, halved and thinly sliced

2 large shallots, halved and thinly sliced

2 large garlic cloves, thinly sliced

Kosher salt and freshly ground black pepper

½ cup dry white wine

5 cups beef stock or bone broth

1 loaf day-old sourdough bread or 1 sourdough baguette

8 ounces Gruyère cheese

½ teaspoon Worcestershire sauce

Finely chopped fresh chives, for garnish

As far as soup goes, French onion has got to be one of my favorites and *this* version only requires one pot. While the key ingredients, caramelized onions and rich beef broth, are still used, here we toss in some shallots and Worcestershire to add a subtle sweetness, tang, and depth. Top with bread and sharp Gruyère cheese and it doesn't get any better. While I love the traditional serving of this soup (in individual bowls or ramekins), it's just as delicious—with less cleanup—if you make it all in one pot.

1. In a medium Dutch oven or braiser, melt the butter over medium heat until glistening. Add your onions, shallots, and garlic. Sauté, stirring frequently (you want caramelization and not burning!), until the onions and shallots are golden brown, 30 to 40 minutes. As you see browning on your onions and shallots, adjust the heat as necessary and add a tablespoon or two of water to deglaze the pan periodically as you caramelize. Season with salt and black pepper.

2. Increase the heat to medium-high, add your white wine, and stir to combine, scraping up browned bits and reducing completely, for 1 to 2 minutes.

3. Add your beef stock and bring to a simmer. Reduce the heat to medium let it warm through and simmer nicely with your onions until thickened, 25 to 30 minutes.

4. Meanwhile, if using sourdough, cut 4 slices ½ inch thick, then cut each in half crosswise. If using a sourdough baguette, cut 8 to 10 slices ½ inch thick. Shred your cheese on the larger holes of a box grater.

5. Toward the last 5 minutes of your soup simmering, position a rack so your soup can be as near the broiler as possible and turn your oven on to a high broil. Taste your soup, and adjust with salt and black pepper if needed. Add your Worcestershire if you want more oomph! I find this gives the soup a deeper umami flavor, some sweetness, and tang.

6. Layer the bread slices over the top of the soup, overlapping as needed, then finish with an even layer of shredded Gruyère.

7. Carefully transfer your pot to the oven to the top rack and broil until the cheese is fully melted, with some charred bits on your bread and some browning on the cheese, 5 to 7 minutes, keeping a close eye on your soup!

8. Remove from the oven, finish with a big heaping garnish of chives, and serve in bowls.

SERVES 4
30 MINUTES

CALABRIAN CHILI TOMATO SOUP WITH PIZZA-ISH CROUTONS

Nothing beats the taste of a cozy creamy tomato soup! It's one of the first meals I learned how to cook at home and I continue to make it often. Here I take this classic dish and spice it up a bit by adding pizza croutons! Welcome this one pot, no-blend spicy chili tomato soup—the Calabrian chili gives this soup a burst of spicy goodness.

If you've never tried Calabrian chilis, they are medium to medium-hot red peppers. The taste is smoky and tangy, especially when blended up in a paste, which is what I'm using here.

PIZZA-ISH CROUTONS

Four ¾-inch-thick slices day-old/stale sourdough bread, roughly torn into small pieces (2 heaping cups torn)

2 tablespoons tomato paste

1 tablespoon extra-virgin olive oil

1 teaspoon dried oregano

1 teaspoon dried basil

Kosher salt and freshly ground black pepper

2 tablespoons finely grated Pecorino Romano cheese, plus more for serving

CALABRIAN CHILI TOMATO SOUP

1 tablespoon extra-virgin olive oil, plus more for drizzling

¼ cup minced shallot (about 1 large)

¼ cup tomato paste

1 heaping teaspoon Calabrian chili paste, plus more to taste

One 14.5-ounce can crushed tomatoes

4 large fresh basil leaves, roughly torn, plus more for serving, or 1 teaspoon dried basil

Kosher salt and freshly ground black pepper

½ cup heavy cream

2 tablespoons unsalted butter

1. **Make your Pizza-ish Croutons:** In a medium bowl, combine the torn sourdough bread, tomato paste, olive oil, oregano, basil, and salt and pepper to taste. Use your hands to toss everything together until the bread is evenly coated in the tomato mixture.

2. In a medium pot, toast the bread mixture over medium-low heat, tossing frequently, until caramelized, crisped, and lightly charred in places, 8 to 10 minutes. Pour back into the bowl, add the Pecorino Romano, and toss to coat. Set aside until ready to serve.

3. **Make your soup:** In the same medium pot, heat the olive oil over medium-high heat. Add the shallot and sauté until translucent and fragrant, 2 to 3 minutes.

4. Stir in the tomato paste and Calabrian chili paste and cook until brick red and caramelized, 2 to 3 minutes. This will develop the flavors and cook down the paste.

5. Pour in the crushed tomatoes. Fill the can with water and pour that in. Toss in the basil and season with salt and black pepper to taste. Bring the mixture to a gentle simmer, then reduce the heat to low and let it simmer for 10 minutes to meld the flavors.

6. Turn off the heat, then stir in cream and butter. Adjust with salt and black pepper to taste and stir well to combine.

7. **To serve:** Pour your tomato soup into bowls, top with the pizza-ish croutons, a drizzle of olive oil, grated Pecorino Romano, and basil leaves.

Serve with Butter Lettuce and Avocado Salad with Uncle Ira's "Good Dressing" (page 80).

SERVES 4
1 HOUR

1 medium leek

4 slices bacon

3 tablespoons unsalted butter

1½ teaspoons smoked paprika

½ teaspoon cayenne pepper

1 cup thinly sliced scallions

Kosher salt and freshly ground black pepper

2 pounds Yukon Gold potatoes, cut into ½-inch cubes

4 cups chicken or vegetable broth

¼ cup sour cream, plus more for serving

½ cup shredded sharp yellow Cheddar cheese

Vegetarian option: Omit the bacon and use vegetable broth.

LOADED BAKED POTATO & LEEK SOUP WITH PAPRIKA BUTTER

You gotta love a good ol' loaded baked potato. But what if we combine that idea with potato and leek soup, and top with paprika butter and all the usual baked potato fixin's? This magical combo of smokiness from the bacon mixed with leeks and scallions, rounded out with the zing of sour cream and loaded with sharp yellow Cheddar, is a game changer.

1. **Equipment:** Bring out your immersion blender or stand blender.

2. Remove any porous outer dark green layers from the leek and cut off the rough dark green top. Cut the leek in half lengthwise, then cut the white and light-green parts crosswise into ¼-inch-thick slices. Transfer to a bowl of water to clean thoroughly. Dry on paper towels.

3. Line a plate with paper towels and have near the stove. Spread the bacon in a single layer in a large cold Dutch oven or pot. Bring the heat up to high and crisp up your bacon, turning occasionally, until golden brown, 7 to 8 minutes. Transfer the bacon to the paper towels to drain and cool. Discard the bacon fat and wipe out the pot.

4. Add your butter, paprika, and cayenne to the pot. Cook over medium-low heat until the butter is melted and the spices are fragrant, 1 to 2 minutes. Spoon 2 tablespoons of the butter into a small bowl and reserve in a warm place.

5. Toss your leeks and ½ cup of the scallions into the pot, seasoning with salt and pepper. Cook over medium heat, tossing occasionally, for 1 to 2 minutes until your leeks are softened.

6. Add your potatoes and cook for another minute. Then add your broth, salt, and pepper, mixing so everything has combined. Bring to a boil over medium-high heat. Reduce to a gentle simmer, cover, and cook over low heat until your potatoes are fork-tender, 20 to 25 minutes.

7. While your potatoes are cooking, crumble the cooled bacon and set aside for topping.

8. Use an immersion blender or stand blender to puree the soup, being careful not to overblend, or your soup will become waxy, tight, and gummy. Once blended, off the heat, stir in your sour cream until completely combined. Season with salt and black pepper, to taste.

9. Ladle your soup into bowls and top with sour cream, bacon bits, the remaining ½ cup scallions, Cheddar, and a drizzle of the reserved paprika butter.

PASTA N' NOODLES BABY!

SERVES 4
30 MINUTES

¼ teaspoon saffron threads

Kosher salt

1 pound short-cut pasta, I'm using lumache

2 tablespoons extra-virgin olive oil

2 pints Sungold tomatoes or cherry tomatoes

4 large garlic cloves, thinly sliced

Freshly ground black pepper

2 tablespoons unsalted butter

¼ cup packed fresh basil leaves

Serve with Roasted Broccolini with Cilantro-Lime Vinaigrette (page 222).

BUTTERY SAFFRON & SUNGOLD TOMATO PASTA

This 30-minute pasta is a summer's dream! I begin making this as soon as I see tomatoes pop up at the farmers' market. The saffron here not only adds a nice orange hue to the pasta, it also gives a fragrant aroma to the Sungold tomatoes. Toss with rigatoni, shell, or lumache pasta, plus a knob of butter and fresh basil, and you have a simple, satisfying pasta meal.

1. Bring a large pot of water to a boil for the pasta.

2. In a mortar and pestle, grind your saffron into a pasty powder. (If you don't have a mortar and pestle, grind between your fingers and place in a cup.) Transfer to a small bowl. Once the pasta water is boiling, take about 2 tablespoons of hot water and pour over your ground-up saffron to bloom.

3. Once the pasta water is boiling, salt generously and add your pasta. Cook until 1 to 2 minutes before al dente according to the package directions. Reserving ½ cup pasta water, drain the pasta.

4. While your pasta is cooking, in a large skillet heat the olive oil over medium heat until shimmering. Add your tomatoes and stir to break them up to make your sauce, 5 to 7 minutes. You can keep some tomatoes whole, but use the back of your spoon to smash down the rest and burst the tomatoes if they need a little more help!

5. Add your garlic and stir for 1 to 2 minutes. Season with salt and black pepper. If your pasta is not ready yet, keep the heat on low.

6. When your pasta is ready, increase the heat under the sauce to medium. Transfer the drained pasta to the tomato sauce. Add your butter and saffron water, tossing to combine. Adjust with pasta water as needed to ensure your pasta is glossy and saucy! Season with salt and black pepper.

7. Turn off the heat and gently toss in your basil leaves. If you have any really large basil leaves, just tear them into a few pieces. Transfer to bowls to serve.

MINTY PASTA WITH HOT ITALIAN SAUSAGE & RED CHARD

SERVES 4
45 MINUTES

Kosher salt

1 pound short-cut pasta, I'm using rigatoni

1 tablespoon extra-virgin olive oil

1 pound hot Italian pork sausage, casings removed

2 bunches of red Swiss chard, with stems

6 large garlic cloves, thinly sliced

Freshly ground black pepper

½ cup grated Parmigiano-Reggiano cheese, plus more for serving

1 cup loosely packed fresh mint leaves, chiffonade-cut

For pasta, I love to use a vegetable, a protein, and lots and lots of pasta water to create a creamy, velvety sauce. Hot Italian sausage has so much depth of flavor with a nice kick. When paired with a hearty vegetable like red chard, it takes this dish to the next level.

If you've never cooked with chard before, it can be a tad bitter, but once cooked, it takes on a sweeter flavor, almost like a more subtle cooked beet. Here, it balances the fatty flavor of the sausage while fresh mint adds brightness to complete our orchestra of flavors.

1. Bring a large pot of water to a boil for the pasta. Once boiling, salt generously and add your pasta. Cook until 1 to 2 minutes before al dente according to the package directions. Reserving 1 cup of pasta water, drain the pasta.

2. While your pasta is cooking, in a large saucepan or Dutch oven, heat the olive oil over medium-high heat until glistening. Add your sausage in large clumps and cook until browned underneath, 3 to 4 minutes. Flip and brown on the other side, another 3 to 4 minutes. Break the meat apart with your spoon into even medium-size crumbles. (You don't want super-small crumbs!)

3. While your sausage is cooking, cut off and discard the bottom inch of your chard stems. Thinly slice the stems and slice the leaves into 1-inch ribbons.

4. Reduce the heat to medium, toss the garlic into the pan and cook until softened, 1 to 2 minutes. Add your chard and continue cooking until the chard has wilted significantly, the garlic is fragrant, and the sausage is cooked through, 5 to 7 minutes. Season with salt and pepper.

5. By this point your pasta should be done. If your pasta is not ready yet, turn your sausage mixture on low until ready to proceed.

6. Add ½ cup of the pasta water to deglaze the pan and fully cook your chard, scraping up any browned bits from the bottom of the pan. Increase the heat to medium-high, add your pasta, and stir everything together, mixing well for 2 to 3 minutes until a nice and glossy sauce is formed.

7. Turn off the heat and add your grated Parmesan and mint. Toss to melt in the cheese and wilt the mint. If it's drier than you would like, adjust with more pasta water. Toss to combine.

8. Serve in bowls and top with more cheese and black pepper.

The sausage, pasta water, and cheese all have a good amount of salt, so keep that in mind when adjusting to taste.

SERVES 4
2 HOURS 45 MINUTES

LAMB BOLOGNESE WITH FENNEL & RICOTTA

2 tablespoons extra-virgin olive oil, plus more for drizzling

1 large yellow onion, finely chopped

1 large fennel bulb, cored, finely chopped, fronds reserved for serving

4 large garlic cloves, thinly sliced

¼ teaspoon red pepper flakes

Kosher salt and freshly ground black pepper

1 pound ground lamb

½ cup dry red wine

One 28-ounce can crushed tomatoes

1 pound pappardelle pasta, or other long flat pasta

⅓ cup grated Parmigiano-Reggiano cheese, plus more for serving

½ cup ricotta cheese

continued...

Bolognese is my comfort food. While beef and pork are delicious options, ground lamb, one of my favorite meat proteins, works perfectly in this recipe that I come back to over and over again. Here we will add fennel (don't forget fronds for serving!) and ricotta into the mix. The ground lamb adds a rich element that is complemented with a dollop of cold ricotta. I'm not sure there's a better pairing.

1. In a large Dutch oven, heat the olive oil over medium heat. Add your onion and fennel and sauté until the vegetables are softened a tad and the onion is translucent but not browned, 5 to 7 minutes.

2. Add your garlic and red pepper flakes and season with salt and black pepper. Do a light toss. It's okay if it's a little dry here—the lamb will add more fat.

3. Add your ground lamb to the pot and bring the heat to medium-high. Cook, breaking up the lamb with a wooden spoon as you toss with the onion, fennel, and garlic. Your lamb should be cooked through and take on a nice brown color around the edges, not too dark, 10 to 15 minutes.

4. Reduce the heat to medium, pour in the red wine, and cook until completely evaporated, about 1 minute. Give your mixture a big pinch of salt.

5. Stir in the crushed tomatoes. Fill the empty tomato can about halfway with water and swirl it around to get all the leftover crushed tomatoes. Add your water to the Bolognese, scraping up the browned bits stuck to the pot, and season with salt and black pepper.

6. Cover the sauce and simmer over low heat, stirring occasionally, until the Bolognese is a deep red-brown color with a texture that is not too watery and just coats the back of the spoon, about 2 hours. If the sauce gets too thick, you can add a splash more water.

7. About 20 minutes before you're ready to serve, bring a large pot of water to a boil for the pasta. Once at a boil, generously salt the water and add the pasta. Cook until 1 to 2 minutes before al dente according to the package directions. Reserving ½ cup pasta water, drain the pasta and set aside in a colander. Also set aside your large pot; you'll use it again later.

8. While your pasta is cooking, stir the Parmesan cheese into your sauce.

PASTA & NOODLES, BABY!

LAMB BOLOGNESE WITH FENNEL & RICOTTA
continued

Serve with Little Gem Caesar Salad with Habanero Dressing & Sourdough Bread Crumbs (page 71).

Toss until melted. Once the sauce is ready, taste and adjust the seasoning as needed. Remove from the heat.

9. In the large pot in which you cooked your pasta, add half the Bolognese sauce and 2 tablespoons of the ricotta cheese and toss to combine over low heat. Add half of the pasta, with pasta water, if the sauce is too dry. Toss until combined, then add the remaining Bolognese, 2 more tablespoons of the ricotta, and the remaining pasta, stirring vigorously to ensure everything is evenly coated.

10. In a small bowl, season the remaining ¼ cup ricotta with salt and black pepper. Drizzle with some extra-virgin olive oil and stir to combine.

11. Transfer your pasta to a serving dish. Top with fennel fronds, additional Parmesan cheese as desired, and a big crack of black pepper. Serve with a dollop of the ricotta on the side.

SERVES 4
15 MINUTES

SPICY PEANUT NOODLES WITH SNAP PEAS & SCALLIONS

14 ounces ramen noodles

½ cup unsalted creamy peanut butter

½ cup low-sodium soy sauce

¼ cup toasted sesame oil

2 tablespoons Chinkiang vinegar or rice vinegar, plus more to taste

2 tablespoons chili oil, plus more for serving

1 teaspoon toasted sesame seeds, plus more for serving

1 pound sugar snap peas

8 scallions

When you want something quick (like 15 minutes) and delicious, this will become your new go-to. The recipe is inspired by the sesame noodles from Din Tai Fung (if you've never tried them before, I highly recommend you do!) and traditional Chinese Dan Dan Noodles, a popular Sichuan dish that combines sesame paste, ground pork, and Sichuan peppercorns.

These noodles are tossed in a vinegary chili oil and peanut sauce, and then mixed with crunchy snap peas and scallions. I often opt to serve the noodles warm, but you can definitely serve this cold, too!

I whip this up for lunch once or twice a week—speedy and easy is the name of the game here.

1. Bring a medium pot of water to a boil. Add your noodles and cook according to the package directions.

2. While your water is boiling and noodles are cooking, in a large bowl, whisk together the peanut butter, soy sauce, sesame oil, vinegar, chili oil, and sesame seeds until you have a smooth paste.

3. Find the tough string at the end of the pod of your snap peas and tear it lengthwise to remove the fibrous part. Thinly slice the snap peas and scallions on a bias.

4. Using tongs, transfer the cooked ramen noodles to the bowl with the peanut sauce (it's okay if some noodle water comes with them). Gradually mix in up to ¼ cup of the noodle water, if needed, to make the noodles glossy and saucy! Toss the noodles until they are evenly coated with the peanut sauce.

5. Add your snap peas and scallions, reserving some scallions for garnish. Adjust with more vinegar to taste. Toss to combine and adjust the consistency with more noodle water if needed.

6. Divide the saucy peanut noodles among bowls. Sprinkle with some toasted sesame seeds, the reserved scallions, and a drizzle of chili oil. Serve warm or cold.

SERVES 4
45 MINUTES

HAZELNUT PESTO BUCATINI WITH SUN-DRIED TOMATO & VINEGAR BREAD CRUMBS

SUN-DRIED TOMATO & VINEGAR BREAD CRUMBS

1 tablespoon sun-dried tomato oil, plus ½ cup drained oil-packed sun-dried tomatoes, finely minced

1 tablespoon distilled white vinegar

½ cup panko bread crumbs

Kosher salt and freshly ground black pepper

HAZELNUT PESTO BUCATINI

Kosher salt

1 pound bucatini pasta

2 cups packed fresh basil leaves

2 cups packed spinach leaves

2 large garlic cloves, smashed and peeled

½ cup roasted skin-on hazelnuts, unroasted works too

½ cup grated Parmigiano-Reggiano cheese, plus more for serving

Freshly ground black pepper

¼ cup extra-virgin olive oil

Every Sukkot, a Jewish holiday in the fall, my Uncle Rouven and Aunt Florette host a dairy-themed menu in their sukkah, an outdoor hut-like structure used for the week of the high holidays. The dinner is filled with bruschetta, creamy pastas, and pizza. One of my favorites every year is their hazelnut pesto with sun-dried tomatoes. It's creamy and tangy from the sun-dried tomatoes, and packs a nice nutty punch from the hazelnuts. Inspired by their pasta, this is a bright and beautiful spinach, basil, and hazelnut pesto that is tossed with bucatini pasta and finished off with crunchy and tangy vinegared sun-dried tomato bread crumbs.

1. **Equipment:** Bring out your food processor.

2. **Make your Sun-Dried Tomato & Vinegar Bread Crumbs:** In a large deep pot, heat the sun-dried tomato oil and vinegar over medium heat until glistening. Add your minced sun-dried tomatoes and panko and cook, stirring occasionally, until golden and toasted, 5 to 7 minutes. Season with salt and black pepper. Remove the bread crumbs from the pot to a bowl to cool. Reserve the pot for the next step.

3. **Cook your bucatini:** Wipe out any excess oil from the pot, fill the pot with water, and bring to a boil for the pasta. Once boiling, salt generously and add your pasta. Cook until al dente according to the package directions. Reserving 1 cup of pasta water, drain the pasta and return it to the pot.

4. **Blend your Hazelnut Pesto:** While your pasta is cooking, in a food processor, combine the basil and spinach and pulse until finely chopped. Then add your garlic, hazelnuts, Parmesan, and salt and black pepper to taste. Pulsing your processor, slowly drizzle in your olive oil until the pesto reaches a thick, emulsified consistency, scraping the sides of the bowl occasionally to evenly combine. You don't want the pesto too watery, more like a thick paste. Set aside.

5. Off the heat, add your pesto and ¼ cup pasta water to the cooked pasta and toss to combine. Continue tossing and adding pasta water as needed until the sauce has thickened and the pasta is glossy and evenly coated. Season with salt and black pepper.

6. **To serve:** Transfer your pasta to a shallow bowl, and top with the sun-dried tomato bread crumbs and more grated Parmesan cheese as desired.

SOJU GOCHUJANG RIGATONI

SERVES 4
30 MINUTES

Kosher salt

1 pound rigatoni (I like mezze rigatoni)

2 tablespoons unsalted butter

4 large garlic cloves, minced

Freshly ground black pepper

2 tablespoons gochujang (Korean chile paste; see note)

¼ cup soju (Korean rice liquor)

1 cup heavy cream

½ cup grated Parmigiano-Reggiano cheese, plus more for serving

I like the O'Food brand of gochujang and used it in this recipe. Just keep in mind that other brands may be a tad sweeter!

We all know (and are equally obsessed with, I'm sure) the classic vodka pasta sauce. But what do you get when you swap in gochujang, a spicy Korean chile paste, for the tomato paste, and soju, Korean rice liquor, in place of vodka? You get a really silky and spicy pasta that, dare I say, will become your new favorite. Top with a dollop of burrata if you'd like to cut the heat a bit!

1. Bring a large pot of water to a boil for the pasta. Once boiling, salt generously and add your pasta. Cook until 1 to 2 minutes before al dente according to the package directions. Reserving about ½ cup of pasta water, drain the pasta.

2. While your water is boiling and pasta is cooking, in a large skillet, melt your butter over medium heat. When lightly bubbling, add your garlic and season with salt and black pepper. Sauté until soft and fragrant without browning, about 1 minute.

3. Add your gochujang and cook it down, stirring often, for 2 minutes; at this point, it should appear deeply red and almost separated. Add your soju, stirring well to combine and reduce slightly, 1 minute more. Then add your heavy cream and simmer the sauce over low heat until it thickens and coats the back of a spoon, 5 to 7 minutes. If your pasta is not ready yet, you can keep your sauce over low heat until ready to combine.

4. Transfer the cooked pasta to the skillet with the sauce. Toss the pasta until it's well coated with the creamy gochujang sauce. Add your Parmesan and adjust with pasta water as needed, stirring constantly over medium-low heat until your pasta is evenly coated and glossy. Season with salt and black pepper.

5. Arrange the sauced pasta in shallow bowls or plates. Serve topped with more grated Parmesan cheese and black pepper.

SERVES 4
30 MINUTES

MUSHROOM MISO MASCARPONE PAPPARDELLE

Kosher salt

12 ounces pappardelle pasta

¼ cup extra-virgin olive oil, plus more as needed

16 ounces oyster and/or maitake mushrooms, roughly torn

Freshly ground black pepper

1 large shallot, finely chopped

2 large garlic cloves, finely chopped

½ cup mascarpone

2 tablespoons white miso

¼ cup finely chopped fresh flat-leaf parsley

Growing up, I wasn't a fan of mushrooms. I didn't really eat them until I was at a bar mitzvah and there was a mushroom sauté station, *yes* a whole table of all types of mushrooms: fried, sautéed, grilled, tossed in pasta, you name it. It was then that I realized mushrooms aren't the problem, it was how I was using them. From that day forward, I was a converted mushroom lover, sautéing, baking, and grilling them often as I was starting to learn how to cook.

So, here's to mushrooms and this umami-filled pasta. Oyster and maitake mushrooms (my two favorite types!) are cooked until golden, mixed with a creamy miso mascarpone mixture, and tossed together with pappardelle pasta. Top with fresh parsley to round it all out.

1. Bring a large pot of water to a boil for the pasta. Once boiling, salt generously and add your pasta. Cook until 1 to 2 minutes before al dente according to the package directions.

2. While you're waiting for the water to boil and your pasta is cooking, in a large skillet, heat the olive oil over medium heat until shimmering. Add your mushrooms and cook, stirring, until they soften a tad and take on a nice deep brown color, 8 to 9 minutes.

3. Season with salt and black pepper. Add your shallots and garlic and continue cooking until fragrant and soft, 1 to 2 minutes. You don't want any color or burning on your garlic or shallots. Adjust with more olive oil, if needed. Bring the heat to low until the pasta is ready.

4. At this point, your pasta should be almost finished. In a small bowl, stir together the mascarpone, miso, and ¼ cup pasta cooking water. Whisk well until completely combined and there are no clumps.

5. Set the skillet over medium heat and use tongs to transfer your pasta into the mushroom mixture, keeping the pasta water on the stove. Give everything a big toss. Then pour in your miso mascarpone mixture and stir well, until a pasta sauce forms; it should be super creamy and velvety. Adjust with more pasta water if your sauce is feeling a little bit too thick. Season with salt (lightly since the miso is already salty!) and black pepper. Give it one more big toss.

6. Turn off the heat, serve in bowls, and top with chopped parsley.

Serve with Ponzu & Togarashi–Marinated Olives (page 38) and Chili Garlic Brussels Sprouts with Furikake (page 218).

SERVES 4
45 MINUTES

2 medium leeks

1 medium head green cabbage (about 2 pounds)

2 tablespoons extra-virgin olive oil

2 small shallots, thinly sliced

6 small garlic cloves, thinly sliced

Kosher salt and freshly ground black pepper

1 pound spaghetti or linguine

4 tablespoons unsalted butter, cubed and cold

½ cup grated Parmigiano-Reggiano cheese, plus more to taste and for serving

Grated zest and juice of 1 small lemon

¼ cup finely chopped fresh chives, for garnish

CARAMELIZED LEEK & CABBAGE PASTA

Leeks and cabbage are caramelized and tossed with pasta, making this a super satisfying and easy dinner. After tasting this hearty meal, you would never know it was packed with vegetables. The sauce comes together in just one pan, with pasta water being used to achieve a silky finish. This is a recipe I run to when the leeks and cabbage are bountiful at the market.

1. Bring a large pot of water to a boil for the pasta.

2. Thinly slice your leeks into rings, place them in a bowl with cold water to wash thoroughly, and rinse until clean. Dry well and set aside. Halve, core, and thinly slice your cabbage.

3. While your water comes to a boil, in a separate large pot or skillet, heat the olive oil over medium until shimmering. Add your shallots and garlic and sauté over medium heat until fragrant and translucent but not colored, 2 to 3 minutes.

4. Add your leeks and cabbage and season with salt and black pepper. Cook down, stirring every few minutes and more often toward the end, until the leeks and cabbage are soft, have shrunk significantly, and have taken on a rich caramelized color, 20 to 25 minutes. If you see browning or burning on your leeks and cabbage, adjust with a tablespoon or two of water to deglaze the pan periodically, stirring and scraping the pan to loosen any browned bits as you continue caramelizing.

5. Meanwhile, once your water is boiling, generously salt and add the pasta. Cook until 1 to 2 minutes before al dente according to the package directions. Scoop out 1 cup pasta water and set aside.

6. Use tongs to transfer the pasta to the skillet (bringing over some pasta water is okay!). Add your cubed butter, Parmesan, and ½ cup of your reserved pasta water, tossing slowly with tongs. Season with salt and black pepper. Your pasta should be glossy, saucy, and cheesy. Add more pasta water and Parmesan, as needed.

7. Turn off the heat and toss the pasta with the lemon zest. Season with fresh lemon juice to taste. Serve garnished with the chives, some grated Parmesan, and a crank of black pepper.

SERVES 4
30 MINUTES

ANCHOVY HARISSA MUSSELS & LINGUINE

2 pounds fresh mussels, rinsed and scrubbed

Kosher salt

1 pound dried linguine

¼ cup extra-virgin olive oil

4 large garlic cloves, thinly sliced

8 oil-packed anchovy fillets

3 to 4 tablespoons harissa paste

1 cup dry white wine

4 tablespoons unsalted butter, cubed and cold

Freshly ground black pepper

⅓ cup finely chopped fresh flat-leaf parsley

I remember the first time I decided to make mussels. I found they are easy to prepare and are actually a pretty affordable seafood option. After feeling adventurous enough to cook them, I quickly became obsessed. They cook in 5 to 6 minutes, and all you really need to do is layer your flavors, cover the pan, and steam them. Riffing off linguine and clams, these are mussels and linguine, amped up with anchovies and spicy harissa paste.

1. Bring a large pot of water to a boil for the pasta.

2. Coming out between the shells of some mussels is a "beard," a feathery looking strand that the mussel had used to attach itself to a surface. To remove, just grip it with your thumb and finger while using your other hand to hold the mussel firm, and strongly pull it out, without cracking the mussel. Set your mussels aside.

3. Once the water is boiling, salt generously and add your pasta. Cook until 1 to 2 minutes before al dente according to the package directions.

4. Meanwhile, in a large skillet, heat the olive oil over medium heat. Reduce the heat, add your garlic, and sauté until softened, 1 to 2 minutes, taking care not to brown.

5. Add your anchovies and allow them to melt, stirring periodically. Stir in your harissa paste and let it cook for a minute or two, until it takes on a darkened red hue. Bring the heat back up to medium, pour in the wine, and simmer to reduce slightly, another 3 to 4 minutes.

6. Now that the sauce is ready, add your cleaned mussels and do a light toss. Cover tightly and cook for 5 to 6 minutes. Check that your mussels have opened; continue to steam for a few more minutes if they have not. Discard any mussels that do not open.

7. Use tongs to transfer your linguine to the skillet, which is still over medium heat. If your pasta is ready before the mussels, transfer it to a colander, reserving your pasta water. Add your butter and toss to combine so the pasta is evenly coated with sauce and your butter has melted, 1 to 2 minutes. Adjust with pasta water, if needed, until glossy and saucy. Season with salt and black pepper.

8. Serve in bowls and top with the parsley.

If you want to store your mussels ahead of time, in a bowl, cover your mussels with a damp paper towel, cover with plastic wrap, and transfer to the fridge.

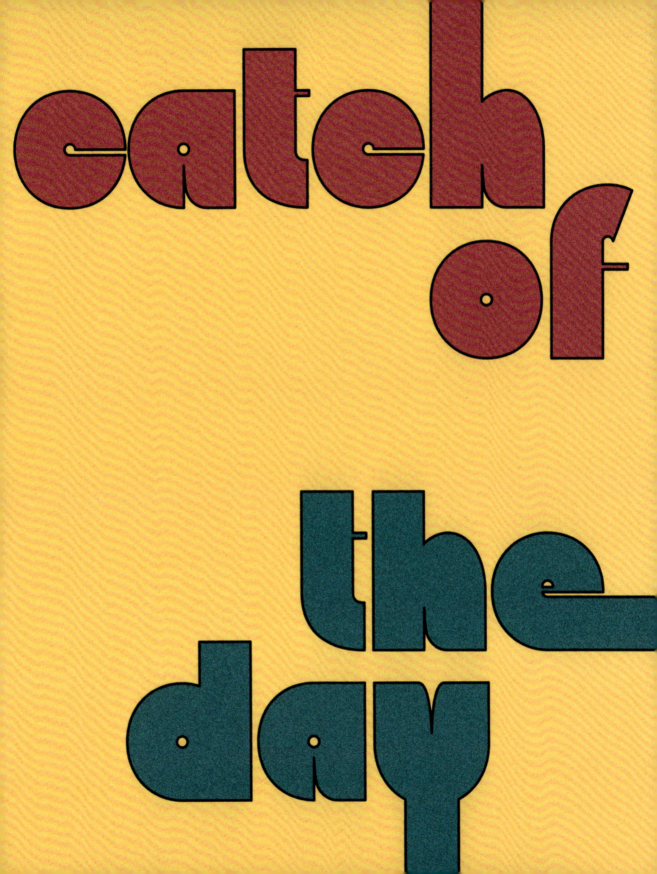

SERVES 4
30 MINUTES

ANCHO CHILE SHRIMP TACOS WITH CREAMY AVOCADO GINGER SALSA

ANCHO CHILE SHRIMP

1 pound medium shrimp, peeled and deveined, tails removed

2 tablespoons neutral oil

1 tablespoon ancho chile powder

½ teaspoon dried oregano, preferably Mexican oregano

½ teaspoon garlic powder

¼ teaspoon dark brown sugar

Kosher salt and freshly ground black pepper

CREAMY AVOCADO GINGER SALSA

1 large avocado, halved and pitted

1 serrano chile, roughly chopped (seeded if you prefer less spicy)

1-inch piece fresh ginger, roughly chopped

2 large garlic cloves, smashed and peeled

½ cup packed fresh cilantro, plus more for serving

¼ cup water, or more as needed

2 tablespoons fresh lime juice (about 1 large lime)

Kosher salt and freshly ground black pepper

FOR SERVING

8 to 10 street corn tortillas

Shredded cabbage

Finely chopped white onion

Lime wedges, for squeezing

Sliced radishes

It is no secret that there is a large variety of taco stands in Los Angeles. The flavorful aromas and smells of grilled meats, like al pastor and carne asada, are one of the unique aspects of Los Angeles food culture. Growing up, for dinners or lunches, we were never far from taco trucks, offering a variety of choices.

Inspired by the classic street taco, these shrimp are seared and finished on corn tortillas. Finely minced cilantro and onions (street taco topping staples) and spicy avocado salsa are also added. Inspired by my Grandma Daisy's ginger avocado chutney, this salsa packs the heat but is balanced out by the crunch of the onions.

1. **Equipment:** Bring out your stand blender or food processor.

2. **Peel and devein your shrimp:** You can purchase peeled and deveined shrimp, but if you don't, here's how to do it: Remove the shell by starting at the head and peel toward the tail. Discard the shells (or save for stock). Using a paring knife, make a shallow cut along the back of the shrimp; you should see a thin, black vein. Use your knife to pull it out and discard. Remove the shrimp tails (if applicable) by gently using your thumb and index finger to twist and pinch off the tail. Discard. Pat dry with paper towels.

3. **Marinate the shrimp:** In a medium bowl, combine the oil, chile powder, oregano, garlic powder, brown sugar, and salt and black pepper to taste. Add your shrimp and toss until combined. Set aside for a few minutes while you make your salsa.

4. **Make your Creamy Avocado Ginger Salsa:** Scoop the avocado into a blender or food processor and add the serrano, ginger, garlic, cilantro, water, lime juice, and salt and pepper. Blend until completely smooth, with a thick salsa-chutney consistency. Adjust with more water and salt, to taste, if needed. Set aside in the fridge until ready to use.

5. **Cook your shrimp:** Heat a large skillet (I like cast-iron here) over medium-high heat until smoking hot. Pour in your shrimp and spread in an even layer. Cook until charred underneath, about 2 minutes. Using a spatula, stir until opaque on all sides, 1 to 2 minutes.

6. **To assemble:** Char your tortillas on the stovetop over the direct flame (or on a dry cast-iron skillet over medium-high heat). Top each tortilla with shrimp, avocado salsa, shredded cabbage, cilantro, and chopped onion. Serve with lime wedges for squeezing and sliced radish on the side.

SERVES 4
45 MINUTES

GOCHUJANG SLOW-ROASTED STEELHEAD TROUT WITH CHERRY TOMATOES

¼ cup gochujang (Korean chile paste)

¼ cup low-sodium soy sauce

¼ cup extra-virgin olive oil

2 teaspoons rice vinegar

Freshly ground black pepper

One 2-pound steelhead trout fillet (or two 1-pound fillets), 1 inch thick

2 cups cherry tomatoes, halved

Thinly sliced scallions, for serving

Lime wedges, for squeezing

Gluten-free option: Swap in coconut aminos or tamari for the soy sauce.

Slow-roasted fish is not only the perfect, easy, entry-level dish, it's also the best set-it-and-forget-it dinner. While the fish roasts in the oven, I like to get goin' on a salad or grain to put together a full meal. You can go so many ways with roasted fish, but for this, I am using gochujang, which we've seen already in Soju Gochujang Rigatoni (page 123). I also love tomatoes, especially cherry tomatoes, and the complex flavors from the spicy gochujang and roasted tomatoes are a perfect pairing. While I am using steelhead, you can easily swap in other fish for this, such as salmon, cod, halibut, or Arctic char.

1. Preheat your oven to 300°F.

2. In a small bowl, whisk together the gochujang, soy sauce, olive oil, vinegar, and black pepper to taste until completely combined.

3. Place your steelhead in a baking dish big enough to fit the fish (if you'd like, line the dish with parchment paper for easy cleanup). Scatter your tomatoes around and over the fish. Pour over your gochujang sauce, making sure it's fully coating the trout and tomatoes. Spoon over any liquid as needed to ensure it's well coated.

4. Slow-roast until the trout flakes easily (or to your desired doneness) and the tomatoes have burst and are slightly caramelized, 25 to 35 minutes, depending on your fillet's size and thickness. Your trout should lose its translucency around the edges (steelhead is orangey hued when raw and cooked). I prefer it a tad medium-rare to medium with an internal temperature of 135°F.

5. Flake the trout in large pieces and arrange on a serving dish (discarding the skin as you transfer) along with the tomatoes. Spoon some of the sauce over. Garnish with thinly sliced scallions and a squeeze of fresh lime juice, serving more lime wedges alongside as well.

SERVES 4
45 MINUTES

GRILLED WHOLE BRANZINO WITH HERBS & LOADS OF LIME

Cassia, a Southeast Asian restaurant in Los Angeles, used to serve an amazing whole grilled branzino. It was filled with tons of fragrant herbs and had the most flaky and tender flesh with crispy skin. That delicious meal is the inspiration for this branzino. A turmeric mixture is added to both the skin and the flesh of the fish, which is then grilled (either directly on the grates, or with a fish grilling basket). I then top it with a pungent and tangy basil and cilantro fish sauce, poured over the crispy fish. While we're using a whole branzino here, you can use branzino fillets, too, or sub in other fish, such as snapper or black bass.

GRILLED WHOLE BRANZINO

2 whole branzino (1 pound each), scaled and gutted

2 tablespoons extra-virgin olive oil

2 tablespoons fish sauce

2 large garlic cloves, grated

1-inch piece fresh ginger, grated

½ teaspoon ground turmeric

Kosher salt and freshly ground white pepper (or freshly ground black pepper)

1 large lime, thinly sliced

A few fresh basil leaves, preferably Thai basil

A few sprigs fresh cilantro

HERB FISH SAUCE

2 tablespoons extra-virgin olive oil

2 tablespoons fish sauce

Grated zest and juice of 1 lime

½ cup finely chopped fresh basil

½ cup finely chopped fresh cilantro

Kosher salt and freshly ground white pepper (or freshly ground black pepper)

If you don't have access to a grill, you can also make this in the oven. Just place your branzino on a parchment-lined baking sheet and roast at 375°F for 15 to 20 minutes.

1. **Grill your branzino:** Preheat your grill to medium-high heat (see note).

2. In a small bowl, stir together the olive oil, fish sauce, garlic, ginger, turmeric, and salt and pepper to taste.

3. Score each side of your fish with shallow diagonal cuts that just pierce the skin. Rub the outside and the cavities of your branzinos with the olive oil/fish sauce mixture, making sure the fish are completely seasoned on all sides. You can use a spoon or a brush or your hands to rub all around the fish. Save your small bowl. Stuff each cavity with the lime slices, basil leaves, and cilantro sprigs.

4. Place the fish either directly on the grill grates (make sure they're clean) or in a fish grilling basket if you have one (then you can flip the fish easily and it prevents sticking!).

5. Grill on each side until the fish has an extremely crispy skin and the flesh turns opaque, 6 to 8 minutes per side. If flipping without a basket, flip carefully with a big spatula or tongs to ensure the skin doesn't stick to the grates. If it's sticking, wait another minute or two before flipping.

6. Once the branzinos are cooked, carefully remove them from the grill and transfer to a serving platter to rest.

7. **Make your Herb Fish Sauce:** While the fish is resting, in a small bowl (you can use the same one as for your marinade), toss together the olive oil, fish sauce, lime zest, lime juice, basil, cilantro, and salt and pepper to taste.

8. Top the fish with your sauce.

SERVES 4
30 MINUTES

SEARED TUNA STEAKS WITH PONZU, CRISPY GARLIC & CUCUMBERS

¼ cup neutral oil

6 large garlic cloves, thinly sliced

Kosher salt and freshly ground black pepper

4 sushi-grade ahi tuna steaks (8 ounces each), about 1 inch thick

2 Persian cucumbers, thinly sliced into rounds

6 scallions, finely chopped or julienned

¼ cup ponzu sauce, plus more to taste

Toasted sesame seeds, for garnish

Chili oil (optional), for drizzling

Steamed white rice, for serving

Ponzu, a Japanese sauce, easily amps up any dish, adding depth of flavor and umami. It's tangy, sweet, salty, and citrusy. When I was first experimenting with fish in the kitchen, I always gravitated toward tuna steaks: I would sear them and always try to mix and match flavors, my favorite being ponzu. Add crunchy cucumbers and crispy garlic to the mix, and you're in for a really special dinner.

1. **Make your crispy garlic:** Line a plate with paper towels and set near the stove. In a large skillet, heat the oil and garlic over medium-high heat until shimmering. Fry until golden brown, mixing constantly, 2 to 3 minutes. Remove the garlic with a slotted spoon and transfer to the paper towels to drain any excess oil. Sprinkle a pinch of salt and black pepper over all the garlic. Keep your skillet on the stovetop and leave any remaining garlicky oil in the pan.

2. **Sear and slice your tuna:** Pat your tuna dry with paper towels and season on all sides with salt and black pepper. Heat your skillet back up over high heat until the oil that was left in the skillet is shimmering. Add your tuna steaks and sear for 2 to 3 minutes per side (for rare, slightly medium-rare which is my preference) or 4 to 5 minutes per side for more medium.

3. Transfer your tuna to a cutting board to rest for 2 to 3 minutes before slicing into ¼-inch-thick slices.

4. **To serve:** Set your tuna on a platter and scatter the cucumbers and scallions over them. Drizzle with enough ponzu sauce to coat everything, finishing with your crispy garlic. Garnish with sesame seeds, a big crank of black pepper, and a drizzle of chili oil (if using). Serve with white rice.

SERVES 4
30 MINUTES

FLAKY WHITEFISH WITH BROWN BUTTER WALNUT VINAIGRETTE

4 whitefish fillets (about 8 ounces each), 1 inch thick and skin-on or skinless, such as halibut, sea bass, or cod

Kosher salt and freshly ground black pepper

8 tablespoons (1 stick/ 4 ounces) unsalted butter

1 cup walnuts, finely chopped

2 small garlic cloves, grated

2 tablespoons fresh lemon juice, plus more to taste

2 tablespoons neutral oil

¼ cup finely chopped fresh chives, for serving

Brown butter has a nutty rich flavor that pairs well with light, flaky fish. Combined with lemon juice and toasted walnuts, you get a crunchy and tangy vinaigrette perfect to drizzle over the top. Serve with finely chopped chives and you have an easy, 30-minute weeknight dinner. You can use a variety of fish, such as halibut, sea bass, or cod. Whitefish tends to work best because it is soft, tender, and buttery when cooked!

1. Pat your fish dry with paper towels and season on all sides with salt and pepper.

2. **Make your brown butter walnut vinaigrette:** In a large skillet, melt the butter over medium heat. Once foamy, add the walnuts and cook, stirring often, until the foam subsides, the butter is golden, and the walnuts are toasted, 6 to 8 minutes. Remove the pan from the heat if you notice the butter is getting too dark. As soon as the proper color is reached, transfer the walnuts and brown butter to a heatproof bowl.

3. Add the garlic, lemon juice, and salt and black pepper to taste to the walnuts and butter. Mix well until combined. Set aside.

4. **Cook your fish:** Using the same skillet, wipe out any walnut bits with a paper towel, add the oil, and heat over medium heat until shimmering. Add your fish and cook, using a fish spatula to push down gently on the top of the fish to form a nice crust, 4 to 5 minutes. Flip the fish and repeat until it has an opaque and flaky center and the internal temperature of the fish is 135°F, 4 to 5 minutes longer.

5. **To serve:** Transfer your fish to a serving platter, drizzling over the brown butter walnut vinaigrette and finishing with a heaping topping of chives, and a squeeze of lemon juice.

SERVES 4
30 MINUTES

STOVETOP MISO HALIBUT EN PAPILLOTE WITH NAPA CABBAGE

½ cup sake

¼ cup low-sodium soy sauce

¼ cup peeled fresh ginger, cut into matchsticks

2 tablespoons white miso

2 large garlic cloves, minced

1 tablespoon mirin

1½ teaspoons rice vinegar

Pinch of freshly ground black pepper

½ small head napa or Savoy cabbage, quartered, leaves separated into small sheets

4 halibut fillets (6 ounces each, ½ inch to 1 inch thick)

FOR SERVING

Steamed white rice

Fresh cilantro sprigs

Toasted sesame oil

Toasted sesame seeds

En papillote is a French term meaning wrapped in parchment, and is a cooking method where food is sealed and steamed in the oven. It's a delicate way to cook fish, with a no-fuss, no-mess process that is foolproof. Although the fish here is wrapped in parchment, it is placed in a covered pan on the stovetop, as opposed to the traditional oven. Instead, the fish is nestled in tightly with a cover, and cooked 'til flaky and tender. A flavor-filled ginger and miso sauce is poured over the halibut and cabbage, resulting in a comforting 30-minute, one-pot meal.

1. In a small bowl, whisk together the sake, soy sauce, ginger, miso, garlic, mirin, vinegar, and black pepper until combined.

2. Cut a piece of parchment paper large enough to wrap all the fillets in one packet. If necessary, fold two sheets together to make a piece big enough to wrap all of the halibut. Place it inside a large skillet or Dutch oven with a cover. Nonstick pans are not recommended for this preparation.

3. Spread your cabbage leaves over the parchment paper. Pour half of your sauce over the cabbage and do a light toss to combine. Add your halibut fillets, skin-side down, on top of the tossed cabbage and season the fish with black pepper.

4. Pour on the rest of the miso sauce. Fold the parchment paper over, starting at one end and making small overlapping folds along all of the edges to create a sealed packet. Tighten the parchment to entirely cover your fish as best you can. Cover with the lid.

5. Set your pan over medium heat and steam for 10 to 12 minutes (depending on the thickness). Turn off the heat and let your fish cool for 4 to 5 minutes, still covered. (We are not opening the cover this whole time!)

6. Remove your lid and carefully open the parchment packet. If your fish doesn't easily flake, cover the pan again and let it sit for a minute or two to finish cooking, until the internal temperature of the fish is around 135°F. Taste the sauce and if it's too salty, add a teaspoon or two of water to dilute.

7. Plate your fish (and any sauce) over steamed white rice and garnish with cilantro sprigs, a drizzle of toasted sesame oil, and toasted sesame seeds.

SERVES 3 TO 4
30 MINUTES

SEARED SCALLOPS WITH DILL CHIMICHURRI & WHITE BEANS

1 pound dry-packed jumbo sea scallops

DILL CHIMICHURRI

⅓ cup finely chopped fresh dill

2 large garlic cloves, minced

1 small shallot, minced

¼ cup extra-virgin olive oil

2 tablespoons white wine vinegar or distilled white vinegar

Pinch of red pepper flakes

Kosher salt and freshly ground black pepper

SCALLOPS

1 tablespoon neutral oil

2 tablespoons unsalted butter

One 15- to 15.5-ounce can cannellini beans, rinsed and drained

You want your scallops as dry as possible for the perfect sear.

I was a scallop skeptic for a long time, especially when they were cooked. They always turned out rubbery and dry, with little to no flavor. As it turns out, it wasn't about the scallops, but more about how I was buying and preparing them. The key is to buy dry-packed scallops and to make sure you get out any moisture prior to cooking them. You also have to make sure you don't overcook them or you won't get that subtle, sweet, and super-tender result. Jammy beans paired with the tenderness of the scallops is the perfect combination. The scallops and beans are rounded out with a zingy, tangy, and aromatic dill chimichurri drizzled over top.

1. **Prepare your scallops:** On the side of each scallop is a muscle particle sticking out slightly. Pull it off and discard. Thoroughly dry your scallops with paper towels and set aside.

2. **Make the dill chimichurri:** In a medium bowl, toss together the dill, garlic, shallot, olive oil, vinegar, red pepper flakes, and salt and black pepper to taste until combined. Refrigerate this vibrant green chimichurri sauce until ready to serve.

3. **Sear the scallops:** In a large skillet, heat the oil over medium-high heat. While your oil is heating up, season all sides of your scallops with salt and black pepper.

4. Add your scallops to the hot pan, in a clockwise formation, making sure not to overcrowd the pan. Do this in batches if needed. Sear the scallops for 2 to 3 minutes on each side, top and bottom, until they develop a nice and golden crust. You don't need to sear the sides of the scallops. For even cooking, flip them according to when they were added. Once you do your first flip, rotate the skillet carefully 180 degrees to allow equal heating on all the scallops.

5. Toward the last minute of cooking, add your butter. As it melts, use a spoon to baste it over the top of the scallops.

6. Reduce the heat to medium-low and transfer your scallops to a serving platter, leaving any remaining butter in the skillet. Add your beans to the skillet, tossing to combine with any leftover butter. Cook until warmed through, 2 to 3 minutes. Season with salt and black pepper.

7. **To serve:** Spoon the beans around the scallops, finishing with a heaping drizzling of your chimichurri.

SERVES 4

12 TO 24 HOURS

GRAPEFRUIT & GINGER CURED SALMON ON BAGELS

¼ cup Diamond Crystal kosher salt

¼ cup granulated sugar

Grated zest of 1 large grapefruit

1 teaspoon black peppercorns, crushed

1 teaspoon finely grated fresh ginger

1 skin-on sushi-grade salmon fillet, about 1 pound, pin bones removed

4 bagels, sliced and toasted

Cream cheese and your favorite toppings, for serving

It is definitely true that your taste buds change over time, and I'm a prime example. Up until high school, I disliked all types of fish, especially smoked salmon. Fast-forward to now, I always find myself craving a bagel, lox, and cream cheese.

Similar to smoked salmon, gravlax is Scandinavian salmon cured with salt and sugar, but not smoked. In this recipe, I am using grapefruit and ginger for the curing process. I love topping it with capers, fresh dill, and thinly sliced red onions, then finishing it off with a generous grind of black pepper. You can reserve your zested grapefruit to squeeze some juice over your bagels when ready to serve.

1. On a sheet pan, lay down a sheet of plastic wrap large enough to wrap the salmon completely. In a medium bowl, combine the salt, sugar, grapefruit zest, black peppercorns, and ginger. Use your hands, if needed, to make sure the mixture is well combined.

2. Place half of this curing mixture in an even layer on the plastic wrap. Set your salmon over it, skin-side down. Spread the remaining curing mixture evenly over the flesh of the salmon. Use your hands if needed to make sure the mixture fully coats the salmon. Cover tightly with the plastic wrap to ensure it's completely sealed.

3. Refrigerate for 12 to 24 hours to cure. I like to place a weight (like a heavy pan or cans) on top to weigh down the salmon and help with the curing process. Don't cure it for more than 2 days, or else it may be too salty!

4. Once the salmon has finished curing, unwrap it and rinse off the curing mixture under cold water. Pat the salmon dry with paper towels and place on a cutting board, skin-side down. Using a sharp knife, starting at one end of your salmon, with your knife held at an angle to the cutting board (almost horizontal to the board), cut into thin slices ⅛ to ¼ inch thick, leaving the skin behind. Store any sliced salmon covered tightly in the fridge for up to 4 days.

5. To assemble the bagels, spread a generous layer of cream cheese on each toasted bagel half. Top the cream cheese with slices of the cured salmon and any of your favorite bagel toppings.

SERVES 4
30 MINUTES

CRISPY-SKINNED SALMON WITH COUSCOUS & ZUCCHINI TZATZIKI

SALMON & COUSCOUS

4 skin-on salmon fillets (6 ounces each)

Kosher salt

2 tablespoons extra-virgin olive oil, plus 1 teaspoon

2 cups pearl couscous

Freshly ground black pepper

3 cups water

1 to 2 tablespoons fresh lemon juice

ZUCCHINI TZATZIKI

1 large zucchini, grated

1 cup whole-milk Greek yogurt

2 large garlic cloves, minced

2 tablespoons finely chopped fresh dill, plus more for serving

1 tablespoon fresh lemon juice, plus more for serving

Kosher salt and freshly ground black pepper

I love crispy-skinned salmon! While I enjoy the simplicity of a slow roast in the oven (see the Gochujang Slow-Roasted Steelhead Trout, page 134), sometimes I crave tender salmon with the crunch of its crispy skin. This one is easy to make and served alongside pearl couscous (which is being made in the same skillet!) and tzatziki, it's my perfect meal.

Traditionally, Greek tzatziki is made with grated cucumbers, but here I'm using zucchini. It works well since it has less moisture, so you don't need to squeeze it out before tossing it with the yogurt sauce.

1. **Season and cook the salmon:** Season the salmon fillets with a pinch of salt and then 2 tablespoons olive oil all over the salmon pieces, rubbing so all the salt and oil are on the salmon.

2. Heat a large nonstick skillet or large nonstick sauté pan over medium-high heat. (Try to use a pan that has a lid available.)

3. Carefully place the salmon fillets into the skillet, skin-side down. Cook, occasionally pressing down gently to crisp the skin, until the skin looks darker in color and the bottom half of the salmon is turning a nice opaque pink-orange color, 7 to 8 minutes.

4. After crisping the salmon skin, flip the salmon and cook on the other side until the salmon reaches your desired temperature, an additional 1 to 2 minutes. I like my salmon around 130° to 135°F. Transfer the salmon skin-side up to a plate.

5. **Make your couscous:** Using the same skillet that your salmon was in, carefully wipe out any leftover oil in the pan with a paper towel. Set over medium-high heat, and add the remaining 1 teaspoon olive oil and the couscous. Toast, tossing occasionally, until just bringing on a light brown color, 1 to 2 minutes. Season with salt and black pepper. Pour in the water, bring to a boil, and cook for 2 to 3 minutes. Lower the heat to a simmer, cover, and cook until the liquid is absorbed and the couscous is tender, 8 to 10 minutes. Turn off the heat, fluff the couscous with a fork, and mix in your lemon juice. Adjust here with more salt, black pepper, and lemon juice as needed.

6. **Prepare your Zucchini Tzatziki:** While your couscous is cooking, in a medium bowl, combine the zucchini, yogurt, garlic, dill, and lemon juice. Season with salt and black pepper to taste.

7. **To serve:** Spread the couscous on a plate and top with your crispy salmon, skin-side up, and tzatziki. Garnish with some fresh dill and squeeze on lemon juice.

Serve with Charred Cabbage with Calabrian Chili Butter (page 209).

GRILLED SUMAC SHELL-ON SHRIMP

SERVES 4
30 MINUTES

1 to 1½ pounds head-off, shell-on shrimp (18 to 20 shrimp)

1 tablespoon extra-virgin olive oil

3 teaspoons ground sumac, plus a pinch for serving

Kosher salt and freshly ground black pepper

1 large lemon, halved

2 tablespoons unsalted butter, softened-ish

Persian Shallot Dip (page 32), for dipping

According to Danny, this recipe is "*chaspeed*," meaning it hits the spot in Farsi. Sumac-spiced shell-on shrimp tossed with butter is a perfect match, and once dipped in Persian shallot dip, it's next level. (Note that for this recipe you'll only need the Persian Shallot Dip—you can skip making the Sumac & Saffron Chili Crisp.) Get messy, peel 'n' eat, and dip!

1. **Split and devein your shrimp:** If you didn't purchase head-off, shell-on shrimp (which are already split up the back and deveined), here's how to split and devein. Using kitchen shears, beginning from the head and stopping where the tail starts, carefully cut through the shell along the back of the shrimp, leaving the shell in place. You should see a thin, black vein. Use your paring knife to pull it out, keeping the shells and tail intact. You can also just use your fingers, or do this with a paper towel. I keep a towel handy to place all the veins on as I go. Pat dry with paper towels.

2. **Grill the shrimp:** Preheat your grill to medium heat. (If you don't have a grill, you can make this the same way on the stovetop using a cast-iron skillet.)

3. In a bowl, toss the shrimp with the olive oil, 2 teaspoons sumac, and salt and black pepper.

4. Place your halved lemon and shrimp on the grill (optional to put onto skewers for easy flipping, but one by one is fine!) and grill for about 3 minutes on one side, flip, and then 2 minutes on the other side. The shrimp should turn orangey-pink, which will signify they're done.

5. Once cooked, place your shrimp in a bowl. Squeeze one charred lemon half over the shrimp and add the remaining 1 teaspoon sumac and the butter. Season with black pepper to taste and toss to combine.

6. **To serve:** Pour the tossed shrimp onto a serving platter (I like to put it on some parchment paper on a plate!) with a little pinch of sumac on top, as well as with your remaining charred lemon half. Serve with the shallot dip for all the shrimp dipping your heart desires!

Serve with Spicy Crushed Cucumber Salad with Feta & Mint (page 72).

Winner, Chicken

Winner, Dinner!

REALLY GOOD ROAST CHICKEN

SERVES 4
1 HOUR

1 whole chicken (4 to 4½ pounds), spatchcocked (see note)

¼ cup extra-virgin olive oil

1 tablespoon Diamond Crystal kosher salt

1 tablespoon freshly ground black pepper

1 tablespoon garlic powder

1 tablespoon smoked paprika

1 tablespoon chili powder

½ cup white wine

2 tablespoons unsalted butter, cubed and cold

1½ teaspoons sherry vinegar

¼ cup finely chopped fresh flat-leaf parsley, plus more for serving

Dairy-free option: Omit the pan sauce entirely, which eliminates the butter.

Serve with Roasted Broccolini with Cilantro-Lime Vinaigrette (page 222), and Butter Lettuce & Avocado Salad with Uncle Ira's "Good Dressing" (page 80).

Everyone needs to know how to cook a basic whole chicken. You can leave the chicken intact, or spatchcock it, which means removing the backbone and flattening the chicken down, which is what we're doing here. This will give the chicken a crispier, more evenly cooked result. You can easily remove the backbone yourself or ask your butcher to do it for you.

The seasoning I'm using here was named "Lindsey's Five Spice Rub" by my sister, Alexa. When we were living at home together I would always season our meals with these five spices: salt, pepper, garlic powder, smoked paprika, and chili powder. At the time, this rub was used to heavily spice roasted sweet potatoes, which I would make on repeat! Feel free to create your own Five Spice Rub: Alter, add, remove, and adjust seasonings as you please.

Use any extra chicken to make Curried Chicken & Celery Salad Sandwiches (page 161) and use any bones from the carcass to make homemade chicken stock.

1. **Roast your chicken:** Preheat your oven to 425°F, on convection if available.

2. Pat your spatchcocked chicken dry with paper towels and place skin-side up in a large deep ovenproof skillet or pan that can be used in the oven and on the stovetop.

3. In a small bowl, combine the olive oil, salt, black pepper, garlic powder, smoked paprika, and chili powder. Mix well until all the spices are incorporated. Pour this all over both sides of your chicken.

4. Roast your chicken uncovered for 40 to 45 minutes. Halfway through the cooking time, rotate the pan front to back to get it evenly browned, and spoon some pan juices over the top of your chicken.

5. Keep roasting your chicken until crispy on the outside, and cooked fully on the inside (at 165°F at the thickest part of the breast).

6. Transfer your chicken to a cutting board and let rest for about 15 minutes. (Reserve the pan and its drippings.)

continued...

REALLY GOOD ROAST CHICKEN
continued

7. **Make a quick pan sauce:** While your chicken is resting, set the reserved pan over medium heat, and add your white wine, scraping up any bits from the bottom of the pan. Cook for 3 to 4 minutes, allowing your wine to furiously bubble and reduce by half. When you run your spatula across the skillet, it should be reduced enough that it should take a moment to flow back into place.

8. Turn off the heat. Add your butter and sherry vinegar, constantly stirring to emulsify. Season with salt and black pepper to taste.

9. Add the parsley and continue to stir to keep your sauce combined. Your sauce should be a thicker texture by now with all the components completely combined. If your sauce breaks—and it's not creamy, thick, and luscious, and the butter has separated—adjust with a splash of water and keep stirring until it comes back together.

10. **To serve:** Cut the wings, legs, and then the breasts. Transfer to a deep platter (so the juices don't spill!) and spoon that saucy pan sauce all over the chicken. Garnish with parsley.

Dry Brining

To add more flavor to your chicken ahead of time, try a dry brine. Dry your chicken well and season with kosher salt and freshly ground black pepper all around your chicken (under the skin, too!), place on a sheet pan, and leave in the fridge, uncovered, overnight. Once you cook your chicken, it will be super juicy, and super crispy since you'll be allowing the chicken skin to dry out overnight uncovered. But, you can 100 percent skip this step—I sometimes do.

How to Spatchcock

Place your chicken breast-side down. Starting on one side of the backbone, use kitchen shears to cut from the tail to the neck of the bird and repeat on the other side of the backbone. Then pull out the backbone. Flip the chicken over so that it is skin-side up and press down hard on the chicken's breast to get it as flat as possible.

SERVES 4
45 MINUTES

ORANGEY CHICKEN PICCATA WITH JAMMY SHALLOTS

2 large or 4 small shallots

⅓ cup all-purpose flour

1 teaspoon Diamond Crystal kosher salt, plus more to taste

½ teaspoon freshly ground black pepper, plus more to taste

2 large or 4 small boneless, skinless chicken breasts (1½ to 2 pounds total)

2 tablespoons extra-virgin olive oil

6 tablespoons unsalted butter, cubed and cold

½ teaspoon red pepper flakes

½ cup dry white wine or chicken stock

1 teaspoon grated orange zest

¼ cup freshly squeezed orange juice (about 1 medium orange)

2 tablespoons capers, drained, plus 1 teaspoon caper juice

Coarsely chopped fresh flat-leaf parsley, for serving

continued...

My husband, Danny, has said that this is one of his favorite dinners I've made for him. Our busy weeknights have me wanting to put in the least amount of effort, but I still want something that is filled with flavor (and uses the fewest dishes possible!). I love a lemony chicken piccata, but this one is special, bringing in the flavors of orange juice and zest, lightened up with sweet and jammy shallots, all made in one pan.

1. Peel your shallots. If you are using large shallots, slice in eighths lengthwise. For small shallots, slice in quarters lengthwise. Keep your shallots as intact as you can.

2. Place your flour in a shallow dish, season with the salt and black pepper, and toss to combine.

3. With a chicken breast flat on the cutting board, make a horizontal cut into the fat side of the breast and slice the breast horizontally in half to make 2 cutlets. You will end up with 4 cutlets. Place each cutlet between two sheets of plastic wrap on a cutting board. Using a meat mallet or small heavy-bottomed pot, pound the chicken to an even ¼-inch thickness. Season both sides of the chicken with salt and black pepper. Dredge each chicken piece in the flour, shaking off any excess.

4. In a large skillet, heat the olive oil and 2 tablespoons of the butter over medium heat until the butter is melted. Working in batches to avoid crowding, add the chicken to the skillet and cook until golden brown and cooked through, 3 to 4 minutes per side. Remove the chicken from the skillet to a plate and set aside.

5. Reduce the heat under the skillet to medium-low. Add the shallots and sauté until they soften, about 5 minutes. Add the red pepper flakes, season with salt and black pepper, and stir constantly for 1 minute longer.

6. Increase the heat to medium and add the white wine to the skillet. Let it simmer for a minute or two, scraping the bottom of the pan to release any browned bits to deglaze the pan. Add 2 tablespoons of the butter, the orange zest, orange juice, capers, and caper juice. Stir to combine and until the butter is melted.

ORANGEY CHICKEN PICCATA WITH JAMMY SHALLOTS
continued

The orange juice almost resembles a sort of orange chicken, so serving this dish with A Pot o' Rice (page 228) would be perfect.

7. Return the cooked chicken to the skillet and add the remaining 2 tablespoons butter. Cook, stirring constantly so the emulsion doesn't break (see note), until the sauce thickens slightly and the chicken is heated, another 2 to 3 minutes.

8. Baste and flip the chicken so it's evenly coated in the velvety sauce. Turn off the heat, taste, and season with salt and black pepper, if needed. Finish with a sprinkle of chopped parsley.

How to Fix a Broken Emulsion

If your sauce breaks, meaning the ingredients are separating and not staying connected, adjust with a splash of water or another tablespoon of butter, bring to a simmer, and stir constantly to bring your sauce back to its emulsified, velvety texture! The sauce should pull back with a spatula and gently fall back down, not too thick and not too watery.

CURRIED CHICKEN & CELERY SALAD SANDWICHES

SERVES 4
15 MINUTES

- 2 cups shredded cooked chicken (roasted, rotisserie or poached), cold
- ½ cup minced celery
- ½ cup minced red onion
- ½ cup thinly sliced scallions
- ⅓ cup mayonnaise
- 2 tablespoons curry powder
- Grated zest and juice of 1 large lemon
- 1½ teaspoons hot sauce, such as Frank's RedHot or Tabasco, plus more to taste
- Kosher salt and freshly ground black pepper
- 8 slices sandwich bread

Celery is an underrated vegetable, but I love its refreshing, crisp texture, and it works really well with shredded chicken. This super earthy and flavor-packed chicken salad is tossed with red onion and scallions, lots of curry powder, and hot sauce. It's crunchy and has a hint of spice from the hot sauce, and all the earthiness and warm flavors you get from curry powder. You can make these sandos with any of your favorite vegetables, like lettuce, tomatoes, or alfalfa sprouts. You can also sub in tuna or eggs for the chicken.

1. In a medium bowl, combine your chicken, celery, red onion, scallions, mayonnaise, curry powder, lemon zest, lemon juice, hot sauce, and salt and black pepper. Gently fold everything together until combined. Adjust as needed to taste with salt, black pepper, and hot sauce.

2. Use right away to make sandwiches with the sandwich bread or cover tightly and set in the fridge for 15 to 20 minutes to allow the flavors to meld together. You can store it in the fridge for up to 3 days.

SERVES 4
30 MINUTES

SKILLET HOT SAUCE & BROWN SUGAR CHICKEN THIGHS WITH FRAZZLED SNAP PEAS

¼ cup low-sodium soy sauce

2 tablespoons hot sauce, such as sriracha or chili garlic sauce

2 tablespoons dark brown sugar

1 teaspoon toasted sesame seeds, plus more for garnish

Freshly ground black pepper

2 pounds boneless, skinless chicken thighs

1 tablespoon neutral oil

8 ounces sugar snap peas, strings removed

Steamed white rice, for serving

Gluten-free option: Swap in coconut aminos or tamari for the soy sauce.

When I was growing up, this dinner was often in rotation. On Sunday, my dad and I would marinate chicken thighs in a sriracha, brown sugar, and soy blend so it would be ready to cook on Monday for a quick 30-minute dinner. The brown sugar adds the perfect sweetness and provides a nice char to the chicken, while hot sauce adds punch. Snap peas are cooked in the same pan, making this a no-fuss, uncomplicated one-skillet dinner. Serve with fluffy white rice!

1. In a small bowl, combine the soy sauce, hot sauce, brown sugar, sesame seeds, and black pepper to taste until the brown sugar is dissolved.

2. Transfer 2 tablespoons of the marinade to a large bowl or bag. Add the chicken and turn to coat. Reserve the rest of the marinade. You can let the chicken sit in the marinade just for the time it takes to cook the snap peas, or you can marinate it for 1 hour or up to overnight in the refrigerator.

3. In a large skillet, heat the oil over medium-high heat until glistening. Add your snap peas and cook and blister for 4 to 5 minutes, stirring occasionally. You want them to just slightly begin to brown in places but still be vibrant green. Remove from the skillet to a plate.

4. Set the skillet over medium heat. Add your chicken thighs, and cook until the internal temperature reaches 165°F, 12 to 16 minutes, flipping over halfway through. If you find the chicken is getting too caramelized and darkened, lower the heat to finish cooking the chicken.

5. Reduce the heat to medium-low. Add the reserved marinade and the snap peas and toss to combine. Cook until the snap peas warm through and your sauce gets saucy, glossy, and just a tad thickened, 1 to 2 minutes.

6. Serve in shallow bowls over cooked white rice, garnished with toasted sesame seeds.

SERVES 4
1 HOUR 15 MINUTES

ALEPPO-BRAISED CHICKEN LEGS WITH BUTTER BEANS & SMASHED OLIVES

10 ounces drained, pitted Castelvetrano olives, plus 2 tablespoons olive brine

½ cup extra-virgin olive oil

2 tablespoons fresh lemon juice, plus more for serving

2 tablespoons freshly squeezed orange juice

2 teaspoons Aleppo pepper

1½ teaspoons Diamond Crystal kosher salt

Freshly ground black pepper

Two 15- to 15.5-ounce cans butter beans, drained and rinsed

6 large garlic cloves, thinly sliced

4 large bone-in, skin-on chicken leg quarters (1½ to 2 pounds)

Oven-braising chicken is a very easy technique that takes little work or skill. Here you add all your ingredients to a baking dish, set it, and forget it. The chicken is oven braised in liquid (in this case, we're using citrus) until it is extremely tender and pretty much falls off the bone. The beans add a rich nutty flavor and the Castelvetrano olives give it a nice buttery texture. A hint of Aleppo is all you need to make this a flavor-packed meal.

1. Preheat your oven to 400°F.

2. Lightly smash your olives with the back of your knife, then roughly chop them.

3. In a small bowl, whisk together the olive brine, olive oil, lemon juice, orange juice, Aleppo pepper, 1 teaspoon of the salt, and black pepper to taste.

4. In a large ovenproof skillet or 3-quart baking dish (just not a sheet pan!), combine the smashed olives, butter beans, and garlic. Pour over half of your Aleppo/olive oil mixture and give your olives, beans, and garlic a good toss.

5. Pat your chicken dry with paper towels. Season on all sides with the remaining ½ teaspoon salt and pepper. Set the chicken legs, skin-side up, on top of the beans and olives. Pour on the remaining Aleppo/olive oil mixture, ensuring it is coating the skin of the chicken.

6. Transfer your skillet or baking dish to the oven and braise until the skin is golden and the thickest part of the leg has reached at least 165°F, 1 hour to 1 hour 15 minutes, rotating the pan front to back halfway through to roast and crisp evenly. At the same time, carefully baste the chicken legs with some of that citrus liquid.

7. Serve with an additional squeeze of fresh lemon juice over top.

SERVES 4
30 MINUTES

FAJITA-RUBBED CHICKEN WITH GRILLED BELL PEPPERS

3 tablespoons extra-virgin olive oil

1 tablespoon chili powder

½ teaspoon ground cumin

½ teaspoon smoked paprika

Kosher salt and freshly ground black pepper

4 large bone-in, skin-on chicken leg quarters, or 5 to 6 bone-in, skin-on chicken thighs (1½ to 2 pounds total)

3 to 4 large bell peppers, a mix of yellow and red

1 large red onion

FOR SERVING

Lime wedges, for squeezing

Corn or flour tortillas, warmed (optional)

Creamy Avocado Ginger Salsa (page 133) or Zesty Crema (page 59) (both optional)

There is nothing like a sizzlin' fajita platter heading toward your table! When you're making it at home, why not change it up by adding crispy, crunchy chicken skin, and jammy bell peppers and onions? I love skin-on for this method, so the skin gets super crispy with the tender chicken, but you can also opt to use skinless chicken breasts if that's your jam. It's brought all together with a squeeze of fresh lime juice. Serve your fajita chicken with warmed tortillas and a creamy avocado salsa or crema.

1. In a medium bowl, mix together 2 tablespoons olive oil, the chili powder, cumin, smoked paprika, and salt and black pepper to taste. Pat your chicken dry with paper towels, add to the spice mixture, and rub to evenly coat, under the skin as well. Set aside.

2. Preheat your grill to medium-high heat. (Alternatively, heat a large cast-iron skillet over medium-high heat.)

3. Quarter your bell peppers lengthwise and deseed them. Slice your red onion into ½-inch-thick rings, keeping the slice intact as best you can. Transfer to a plate, bag, or tray and season with the remaining 1 tablespoon olive oil and salt and black pepper. Toss gently to coat.

4. Place the peppers, onion, and chicken on the preheated grill, chicken skin-side down. Grill, flipping and checking occasionally for flare-ups, until the chicken skin is deeply charred, the internal temperature reaches 165°F, and the vegetables are charred and softened, 10 to 14 minutes. (If you are doing this in a cast-iron, the times and tests for doneness are the same.)

5. Transfer your peppers, onions, and chicken to a platter, and add lime wedges. Serve with tortillas, salsa, and crema (if using).

SERVES 4
1 HOUR 15 MINUTES

1 whole chicken (about 4 to 4½ pounds), cut in half, backbone removed

¼ cup extra-virgin olive oil, plus more for drizzling

4 teaspoons cayenne pepper

2 teaspoons Diamond Crystal kosher salt, plus more to taste

2 teaspoons freshly ground black pepper, plus more to taste

4 large carrots, plus roughly torn carrot tops

1 large lemon, cut into wedges

½ cup cayenne hot sauce, preferably Frank's RedHot

2 tablespoons honey

2 tablespoons cold unsalted butter

HONEY BUFFALO GLAZED CHICKEN WITH SHAVED CARROTS

We all love a classic Buffalo wing (obvi), but how about glazing a cayenne-roasted chicken with honey Buffalo sauce for a showstopping main? Serve alongside shaved carrots to complement the spiciness and tang of the chicken and provide a delicious crunch. I highly recommend pairing this with the Steakhouse Wedge Salad with Gorgonzola Dressing & Bacon Bread Crumbs (page 76), using any extra dressing for dipping.

1. Preheat your oven to 425°F, on convection if available. Line a large sheet pan with parchment paper.

2. **Season and roast the chicken:** Pat your chicken dry with paper towels and place skin-side up on the lined pan. In a small bowl, mix together the olive oil, cayenne, salt, and black pepper. Pour the mixture over the chicken on the baking sheet. Massage in the seasonings all over both sides of the chicken, flipping to mix well in all parts.

3. Transfer your chicken to the oven and roast, uncovered, for 40 to 45 minutes. Rotate the baking sheet front to back halfway through the cooking time to get it evenly browned. Your chicken skin should be crispy, with the exterior color a golden red hue from the cayenne pepper.

4. **Make the shaved carrots:** While your chicken is roasting, use a vegetable peeler to peel the carrots lengthwise into ribbons. Transfer to a bowl and toss with salt and black pepper to taste, a drizzle of olive oil, and a squeeze of fresh lemon juice (reserve the remaining lemon wedges for serving). Refrigerate until ready to serve.

5. **Prepare your honey Buffalo glaze:** In a small saucepan, combine the hot sauce, honey, and salt and black pepper to taste. Cook over medium-low heat until the sauce thickens to a glaze and the honey is incorporated, 2 to 3 minutes. Turn off the heat, add your butter, and stir to combine and melt. Keep your glaze on the stovetop until the chicken is ready.

6. Remove your chicken from the oven and spoon or brush half of your glaze over the chicken. Return to the oven and roast until 165°F at the thickest part of the breast, an additional 6 to 10 minutes.

7. Remove from the oven and brush the remaining glaze over the chicken.

8. **To assemble:** Set the chicken on a large plate and garnish with roughly torn carrot tops. Serve the shaved carrots alongside, with lemon wedges for squeezing.

SERVES 4
45 MINUTES

GARLIC & OLD BAY BRICK CHICKEN WITH SCHMALTZY BABY POTATOES

4 large bone-in, skin-on chicken thighs (1½ to 2 pounds)

Kosher salt and freshly ground black pepper

2 tablespoons extra-virgin olive oil

1½ pounds baby potatoes, halved

2 tablespoons Old Bay seasoning, plus more for sprinkling (see note)

6 large garlic cloves, minced

¼ cup finely chopped fresh flat-leaf parsley

Grated zest and juice of ½ large lemon, plus other ½ in lemon wedges, for squeezing

Chicken and potatoes are a classic combo in most homes, and everyone has a rendition based on their own culture and upbringing. In our house, my dad would roast chicken and potatoes with thyme, garlic powder, ginger, salt, pepper, and brown sugar. Using Old Bay seasoning and garlic, I've put my spin on it.

The "brick" method is used for the chicken, and I mean that literally! A brick is placed on top of the chicken as it cooks, helping it become super crispy; then we'll add potatoes into all the shmaltzy goodness and finish in the oven. Did I mention, this is all done in one skillet?

1. **Equipment:** Get out a brick and wrap in aluminum foil. Or you can use any heavy-bottomed pan, weight, or heavy press.

2. Preheat your oven to 400°F.

3. Pat your chicken dry and season with salt and black pepper, on and under the skin.

4. In a large cast-iron or other ovenproof skillet, heat the olive oil over medium-high heat until smoking. Add your chicken thighs, skin-side down. Set your brick on the chicken and cook, char, and crisp for 6 to 8 minutes. Flip the chicken, set the brick on top, and cook for 2 to 3 minutes longer. Transfer to a plate; at this point, the chicken won't be fully cooked.

5. Add your potatoes and 1 tablespoon Old Bay to the skillet and toss to combine. Cook the potatoes over medium-high heat, stirring periodically, until they start to develop a golden crust, 4 to 5 minutes. Add your minced garlic and do a light toss to combine.

6. Return the chicken to the pan, skin-side up, and top with the remaining 1 tablespoon Old Bay seasoning.

7. Transfer the skillet to the oven and roast until the chicken is cooked to an internal temperature of 165°F, 10 to 15 minutes. If the potatoes need more time, you can remove the chicken and continue roasting the potatoes until they are tender and golden.

8. While your chicken and potatoes are in the oven, in a small bowl, toss together the parsley, lemon zest, lemon juice, a pinch of salt, and a big crank of black pepper. Toss to combine.

9. Serve the crispy chicken and potatoes with a sprinkling of Old Bay, your parsley topping, and lemon wedges for squeezing.

If you've never had Old Bay seasoning before, it is a deeply savory blend of celery salt, paprika, mustard, and black pepper, oftentimes used to season lobster rolls, crab cakes, and shrimp.

Serve with Cucumber, Cantaloupe & Tomato Salad with Ranch-Ish Dressing (page 84).

SOMETHING DELICIOUS

SERVES 4
30 MINUTES

2 large or 4 small boneless, skinless chicken breasts (1½ to 2 pounds total)

Kosher salt and freshly ground black pepper

1 cup panko bread crumbs

¼ cup finely chopped fresh dill

¼ cup finely chopped fresh basil

1 tablespoon toasted sesame seeds, plus more for topping

1 large egg

Neutral oil, for shallow-frying

Serve alongside Endive & Whole-Grain Mustard Salad (page 75). Pair with Brown Butter & Miso Cinnamon Babka (page 241).

CRISPY SESAME & HERB CHICKEN SCHNITZEL

Schnitzel was a childhood staple for me and still is to this day. There is not a family holiday or gathering where it is not on the table. Traditionally from Austria, schnitzel is made with a thinly pounded veal cutlet coated with bread crumbs and fried. In our family, it is always made with chicken. My Aunt Nina always adds a large amount of fresh herbs, like dill and parsley, to liven and brighten up the chicken, and that's something that I now always include in mine. She is beauty, she is grace!

1. If starting with 2 large chicken breasts, you first need to cut them into cutlets. With a chicken breast flat on the cutting board, make a horizontal cut into the fat side of the breast and butterfly the breast horizontally in half to make 2 cutlets. Place each chicken breast or chicken breast cutlet between two sheets of plastic wrap on a cutting board. Using a meat mallet or small heavy-bottomed pot, pound the chicken to about ¼-inch thickness. Season with salt and black pepper on all sides.

2. **Set up your breading station with two shallow bowls or plates:** In one bowl/plate, toss together the panko, dill, basil, sesame seeds, and salt and black pepper to taste. In the second bowl/plate, beat your egg until the yolk and white are completely combined. Season with salt.

3. Pour ½ inch of oil into a large skillet and heat over medium heat to 350°F, using an instant-read thermometer as a guide. You don't want the oil too hot or your panko will burn before your chicken is properly cooked.

4. Dredge your seasoned chicken first in the egg mixture, letting any excess drip off, then in the panko mixture, making sure the chicken is evenly coated.

5. **Shallow-Fry Your Schnitzel:** Line a plate with paper towels and set near the stove. Working in batches to not crowd the skillet, carefully add the breaded chicken and cook, turning once, until your chicken is golden brown and fully cooked inside, 2 to 3 minutes, per side. Transfer your chicken to the paper towels to drain excess oil. Sprinkle a pinch more toasted sesame seeds over the chicken when they are on the paper towel and still hot!

SERVES 4
2 TO 9 HOURS

1 whole chicken (4 to 4½ pounds), cut in half, backbone removed

Kosher salt and freshly ground black pepper

1 cup whole-milk Greek yogurt

½ cup pomegranate molasses

½ cup extra-virgin olive oil

Serve with Beet & Peach Salad with Burrata, Toasted Hazelnuts & Green Goddess Vinaigrette (page 79).

POMEGRANATE YOGURT MARINATED GRILLED CHICKEN

Something absolutely glorious happens when you marinate chicken in yogurt. The acid in yogurt helps tenderize chicken, making it the most deliciously moist (no, I'm not afraid to say that word) grilled chicken you could ever eat. As a bonus, you also experience a tangy yogurt flavor that chars and crisps beautifully on the grill. Pomegranate molasses in the marinade gives a sweet and tart finish to the chicken. Don't forget to save some of the pomegranate yogurt for dipping!

1. Season your chicken on all sides with salt and black pepper.

2. In a large bowl, whisk together the yogurt, pomegranate molasses, olive oil, and salt and pepper to taste. Transfer ½ cup to a small bowl. To the large bowl, add the chicken and mix to coat. Cover both bowls and refrigerate for 1 to 8 hours. This helps enhance the flavors and tenderize the chicken.

3. When ready to grill, preheat your grill to two-zone, medium-high heat. Place your chicken halves on the hot side of the grill, skin-side down, and grill, turning once, until nicely charred, about 8 to 10 minutes per side.

4. Move the chicken, skin-side up, to the indirect heat side of the grill, or if you don't have a grill for two-zone cooking, reduce the heat to low. Close the lid of the grill and continue to cook until the breast reaches an internal temperature of 165°F, 20 to 25 minutes.

5. Remove the chicken to a cutting board to rest for 5 to 10 minutes. Slice the wings from both halves of the chicken, then separate your wings, thighs, and breast. Remove the bone from the breast, then slice the meat.

6. Transfer the chicken pieces to a platter and serve with the reserved yogurt marinade on the side for dipping.

meat me half-way

SERVES 4
30 MINUTES

SPICED LAMB MEATBALLS WITH FETA, TOMATO & CUCUMBER SALAD

SPICED LAMB MEATBALLS

1 pound ground lamb

¼ cup panko bread crumbs

1 large egg

1 tablespoon extra-virgin olive oil, plus more for searing

½ teaspoon Diamond Crystal kosher salt

½ teaspoon freshly ground black pepper

¼ teaspoon ground cumin

¼ teaspoon ground coriander

¼ teaspoon smoked paprika

FETA, TOMATO & CUCUMBER SALAD

4 medium tomatoes

2 Persian cucumbers

4 ounces feta cheese, thinly sliced

1 tablespoon extra-virgin olive oil

Juice of ½ large lemon, plus wedges for serving

Kosher salt and freshly ground black pepper

Serve with Lemony Couscous with a Kick (page 229).

When I need dinner on the table in less than 30 minutes, I always gravitate toward these stovetop lamb meatballs. During the summer, when tomatoes are at their peak, these meatballs pair beautifully with this feta, tomato, and cucumber salad. The tangy and salty flavors from the feta give the perfect balance with the meatballs, tomatoes, and crunch from the cucumbers.

1. **Make your Spiced Lamb Meatballs:** In a large bowl, combine your lamb, panko, egg, olive oil, salt, black pepper, cumin, coriander, and smoked paprika. Mix well to combine, being careful not to overmix (or else it gets too tough, and we want tender meatballs).

2. Line a sheet pan with parchment paper. Divide the mixture into 12 equal portions (about 2 heaping tablespoons each) and form into meatballs with your hands. Place on the lined baking sheet.

3. In a large skillet, heat a drizzle of olive oil (about 1 teaspoon since the fat from the lamb will make a lot of oil) over high heat until piping hot. Carefully add your meatballs in a single layer, and cook, turning frequently, until they are nicely browned on all sides, 5 to 6 minutes.

4. Reduce the heat to medium-low and finish cooking your meatballs, stirring often, until fully cooked and they reach an internal temperature of 165°F, 3 to 5 minutes.

5. **Make your Feta, Tomato & Cucumber Salad:** While your meatballs are browning, cut your tomatoes into ½-inch wedges. Halve your cucumbers lengthwise and slice crosswise into ½-inch half moons. In a medium bowl, toss together the tomatoes, cucumbers, feta, olive oil, lemon juice, and salt and pepper to taste. Set aside in the refrigerator until ready to serve.

6. **To serve:** Divide the salad among bowls and add the spiced meatballs. Serve with lemon wedges, for squeezing.

SERVES 4
1 HOUR 30 MINUTES

ONION BUTTER KEBAB KOOBIDEH WITH RADISHES & HERBS

¼ teaspoon saffron threads (optional)

1 large yellow onion

2 small garlic cloves, peeled but whole

1 pound ground beef (80/20)

½ teaspoon ground turmeric

Kosher salt and freshly ground black pepper

2 bunches of radishes, washed and thinly sliced

1 teaspoon sumac, plus more for serving

2 cups mixed fresh herbs, such as Thai basil, mint, and fresh flat-leaf parsley

Grated zest of ½ large lemon, plus lemon wedges, for serving

2 tablespoons unsalted butter

Serve with sangak, lavash, or pita

Loghmeh in Farsi means the perfect bite, and this kebab koobideh is exactly that. If you're not familiar with koobideh, it is a Persian style of kebab made with ground chicken, beef, or lamb. The ground meat is tossed with minced onions (squeezed as dry as possible), which helps keep the koobideh tender and moist, but not wet or soggy. The liquid drained from the onions is then mixed with butter and brushed over the kebabs during cooking.

The skewers are grilled directly on the flames (or coals), not on your grill grates, which helps keep all the moisture locked in to get the most golden brown char. (There are also instructions below for grilling without skewers or cooking them in the oven.)

Oftentimes when you go eat at a Persian restaurant, they'll bring you an appetizer called *sabzi khordan*: radishes, onions, and fresh herbs to eat with bread and feta (or butter). I wanted to make a tossed herby salad that is inspired by that appetizer, to be served alongside the koobideh and sangak, a popular Persian bread. You place the koobideh directly on top of the bread, so the juices seep into the bread, adding so much flavor with each bite. Danny first showed me this way of eating koobideh and I was immediately hooked. I may even prefer it on bread rather than with rice. To make the perfect bite, take some bread, wrap it around your koobideh, and top with your radishes and herbs, close up as best you can, and take your first bite!

1. **Equipment:** You will need 8 flat metal skewers that are 1 inch wide and about 23 inches long. You also need a grill that can be set up for direct heat, ideally a charcoal grill. The skewers need to be over as direct a heat as possible. For most grills, you can remove the grates and position the skewers carefully over the direct flame. (See the note for cooking in the oven.)

2. **Bloom your saffron (if using):** In a mortar and pestle, grind your saffron into a pasty powder. (If you don't have a mortar and pestle, just grind between your fingers and place in a cup.) Add 2 small ice cubes or 1 tablespoon ice water to the mortar (or the cup). Allow the ice to melt completely, which will bloom your saffron, adding flavor, aroma, and color; it should be a vibrant, almost electric orange. Now you have your saffron water!

continued...

SOMETHING DELICIOUS

ONION BUTTER KEBAB KOOBIDEH WITH RADISHES & HERBS
continued

3. **Make your koobideh mixture:** Line a microwave-safe bowl with cheesecloth (or a thin kitchen towel). Grate your onion and garlic on the small holes of a box grater into the cheesecloth. (I like to pulse this until super smooth in a food processor, so you can do that if you have one.) Wrap and squeeze to take out all the moisture, reserving the onion liquid in the bowl beneath. You want the onions as dry as possible.

4. In a large bowl, combine the beef, saffron water (if using), drained onion and garlic, turmeric, and salt and black pepper. Toss really well with your hands until fully incorporated, and don't overmix. Set aside in the fridge, uncovered, for at least 30 minutes, and up to overnight covered. If you are putting the koobideh mixture in the fridge overnight, cover your onion water and transfer to the fridge until ready to cook.

5. **Prepare your radishes and herbs:** While your beef is chilling, in a small bowl, toss together your sliced radishes, sumac, fresh herbs, lemon zest, and salt and black pepper to taste. Toss to combine and set in the fridge until ready to serve.

6. **Make your onion butter:** Before you are ready to cook your beef, add the butter to your reserved onion liquid and melt in the microwave or on the stovetop. Season with salt and stir to combine. Set aside.

7. Preheat your grill to medium-high heat. (Or preheat your oven to 400°F.)

8. Fill a small bowl with cold water. Divide your meat mixture into 8 equal portions and form each roughly into an 8- to 9-inch long sausage-like shape. Hold a portion of meat in your nondominant hand and set the skewer over it. Gently push the skewer down into the meat and wrap the meat around it, then spread the meat evenly out along the skewer. You want the meat pretty thin, flat, and stuck to the skewer. Dip your fingers in the cold water as you form the koobideh, which will help the meat stick to the skewer. Use your thumb to press crosswise grooves the length of the meat. Be patient as you place your beef on the skewer; if you feel that it is not sticking properly, just remove it and try again, using pressure to stick it tightly on the skewer. If your meat gets warm, refrigerate before continuing; it's easier to form and grill the skewers with cold meat, so take the few minutes to refrigerate the meat at any point if you need to.

To grill your koobideh directly on the grates without skewers, form the meat into the shape of a sausage, then grill for 2 to 3 minutes to allow the meat to firm up to prevent sticking on the grates. Flip every minute until cooked. A few minutes before the end of grilling, brush over the onion butter on all sides of the koobideh.

To cook the skewers in the oven, position a rack in the top position and preheat the oven to high broil. Arrange the skewers on a rack set in a sheet pan and broil until fully cooked, and charred, 8 to 9 minutes, flipping halfway.

Serve with Persian Shallot Dip (page 32) and Spicy Crushed Cucumber Salad with Feta & Mint (page 72) for the ultimate koobideh feast.

9. **Grill your koobideh:** Place the koobideh skewers over the hot coals and grill for 8 to 9 minutes, flipping every 30 seconds to 1 minute, until they are charred and fully cooked. (If using a gas grill, cover between flips.) Once you see some charring and the meat is firm, a few minutes before the end of grilling, brush the koobideh on all sides with the onion butter as you keep flipping the beef.

10. When the beef has a couple of minutes to go, place your bread on the grates to toast gently. If you aren't using the grill grates, then you can toast the bread on your stovetop over the flame. Transfer to a platter.

11. **To serve:** Using another piece of bread (one that is still soft and not toasted), carefully pull your beef off the skewers directly on top of your toasted bread on the platter, so the juices can soak into the bread (the best part!). Spread another layer of your onion butter to gloss the top of the koobideh. Finish with a big handful of your radishes and herbs alongside your bread and beef. Sprinkle sumac over the koobideh and serve with lemon wedges for squeezing.

SERVES 2 OR 4
45 MINUTES

SMASH BURGERS WITH SECRET SAUCE

SECRET SAUCE

⅓ cup mayonnaise

¼ cup ketchup

2 tablespoons finely chopped pickled jalapeños, plus 2 teaspoons pickled jalapeño juice

Kosher salt and freshly ground black pepper

Pinch of sugar

SMASH BURGERS

4 tablespoons unsalted butter (optional), at room temperature

2 or 4 hamburger buns, preferably potato buns

1 pound ground beef (80/20)

Neutral oil, for searing

Kosher salt and freshly ground black pepper

4 slices American cheese

Your favorite burger toppings, such as iceberg lettuce (shredded or in slabs), sliced tomato, and pickled jalapeños or bread and butter pickles

This makes four single smash burgers or two double-doubles.

When I want a burger, I want a smash burger! Crunchy and crispy edges on a buttered potato roll with American cheese (nonnegotiable for me). Everyone has their go-to Secret Sauce, and mine is made with pickled jalapeños and jalapeño juice, which make it extra tangy, extra briny, with a kick of spice. A burger is really a choose-your-own-adventure type of deal when it comes to toppings, but I love shrettuce, tomatoes, and bread and butter pickles!

1. **Make your Secret Sauce:** In a small bowl, mix together the mayonnaise, ketchup, pickled jalapeños, jalapeño juice, and season with salt, black pepper, and sugar until well combined. Cover and refrigerate until serving.

2. **Make your Smash Burgers:** Preheat a large griddle or large stainless steel or cast-iron skillet over medium-high heat.

3. Spread your softened butter (if using) all over the interior of the buns. Working in batches if necessary, set the buns cut-side down on the griddle or in the skillet and toast until golden brown, 2 to 3 minutes. Transfer to a platter until serving. Keep your griddle or skillet on the heat.

4. Divide the ground beef into 4 equal portions and roll each portion into a ball.

5. Bring the griddle or skillet up to high heat. Add a drizzle of neutral oil until smoking. Working in batches if necessary, place a ball of beef on the hot skillet. Use a burger press or a metal spatula to press the ball down with even weight to create a super-thin patty. Season with salt and black pepper. If you're not getting the smash you're looking for, use a spatula to press down, and then use another spatula or the back of a big spoon to force the spatula down on the patty.

6. Cook the burgers until a crispy, charred, deep-brown crust forms underneath, 3 to 4 minutes. I like mine quite charred, so I will wait until the outer edges get a golden brown and crispy. Gently slide the spatula under the patties to flip, and season the other side with salt and black pepper. Place a slice of American cheese on top, and cover with a skillet lid to melt and steam the cheese completely, about 30 seconds. Set aside your cheesy patties on the platter next to the toasted buns.

7. **To assemble your burgers:** Add secret sauce on the top and bottom buns, set one or two cheesy patties on top of the bottom bun depending if you want a single or double-double, and then add any toppings of choice. Cover with the top bun and serve immediately.

SERVES 2
1 HOUR

STEAK & POTATOES FOR TWO WITH ASPARAGUS & BAGNA CAUDA

One 1-pound steak, such as hanger, New York, bavette, 1 inch thick

1 tablespoon neutral oil

Diamond Crystal kosher salt, to taste, plus 2 tablespoons

Freshly ground black pepper

1 pound baby potatoes

1 bunch of asparagus

4 tablespoons unsalted butter, cold and cubed

4 anchovy fillets

2 large garlic cloves, smashed and peeled

Flaky salt, for serving

Bagna cauda is a classic appetizer that's popular in parts of Italy and France. Its name means "hot bath," a reference to warmed olive oil and butter with fresh garlic and anchovies. It's like fondue but without cheese, oftentimes served with assorted vegetables. I'm riffing off of that here by pairing steak with crunchy asparagus and soft, pillowy, tender potatoes, and instead of making a classic bagna cauda in a pot, I make a pan sauce in the same skillet as the seared steak.

1. Take your steak out of the refrigerator and allow it to stand at room temperature for at least 15 and up to 30 minutes. Rub your steak with the oil and season generously on all sides with salt and black pepper. Line a sheet pan with parchment paper and place a wire rack on top. Set aside for later.

2. **Cook your potatoes and asparagus:** While your steak comes to room temperature, in a medium pot, combine your baby potatoes, cold water to cover, and 2 tablespoons kosher salt. Bring to a boil over medium-high heat. Reduce to a gentle simmer and cook until fork-tender, 10 to 15 minutes.

3. **Prepare your asparagus:** Meanwhile, you can either cut 2 inches off of the asparagus bottoms or snap the ends off. To snap, hold the asparagus with a hand at each end and bend the asparagus until the end toward the stem snaps off naturally. When the potatoes have 3 to 4 minutes to go, add the asparagus and blanch until vibrant green and still with a bite to it. You want it crunchy outside and soft inside. Drain both your asparagus and potatoes. If your steak isn't ready yet, return the vegetables to the pot. Cover with the lid until ready to serve.

4. **Cook your steak and make the bagna cauda sauce:** While your potatoes and asparagus are boiling, heat a medium cast-iron skillet over high heat. Let your pan get really hot and slightly smoking.

5. Carefully place the steak into the skillet away from you and sear for 3 to 4 minutes on each side, until a thick crust forms. Press down occasionally with tongs to ensure your steak is getting an even crust. Continue turning your steak occasionally every few minutes until the steak registers an internal temperature of 115° to 120°F. It'll finish cooking to your desired doneness when we make the pan sauce.

continued...

STEAK & POTATOES FOR TWO
WITH ASPARAGUS & BAGNA CAUDA
continued

Serve with Scallop & Radish Crudo with Chile & Citrus (page 37) and Blackberry Maple Bourbon Old-Fashioned (page 253).

6. Reduce the heat to medium-low. Add your butter, anchovies, and garlic. Carefully baste your steak, continuing to turn it, until it reaches your desired doneness, preferably 125° to 130°F for medium rare, 1 to 2 minutes. Remove the skillet from the heat and transfer your steak to the wire rack to rest for at least 10 minutes, leaving the bagna cauda in the pan.

7. Once your steak has rested, slice diagonally against the grain. Keep in mind that your bagna cauda is already plenty salty from the anchovies, so no need to season additionally here!

8. **To serve:** Arrange the asparagus and potatoes on a platter and season with flaky salt and pepper. Set the sliced steak on the platter and finish by pouring over your bagna cauda pan sauce.

SERVES 4 TO 6
3 TO 4 HOURS

AUNTIE NINA'S SPICY SLOW-BRAISED BEEF CHITANNI

2 pounds beef stew meat, cut in 1-inch cubes

Kosher salt and freshly ground black pepper, plus ½ teaspoon Diamond Crystal Kosher salt

2 large yellow onions

1-inch piece fresh ginger

5 large garlic cloves

1 tablespoon neutral oil, plus more as needed

1 teaspoon cayenne pepper

1 teaspoon garam masala

1 teaspoon curry powder

½ teaspoon ground cumin

½ teaspoon ground turmeric

One 6-ounce can tomato paste

1 tablespoon tamarind paste

1½ cups water

FOR SERVING

A Pot O' Rice (page 228)

Chopped fresh cilantro

continued...

Auntie Nina's chitanni is a staple in my family and is always the most requested meal. It is similar to a braised beef masala curry stewed with LOTS of caramelized onions. The secret ingredient is tamarind paste, which offers an indescribable tangy, tart flavor.

So what does the word chitanni—or chitarnee, as it is often spelled—actually mean? Honestly, I have no idea. While I have asked all my family members and tried to research the meaning online, I have still come up short! What I did find was some Indian-Jewish Sephardic cookbooks at my Grandma Daisy and Auntie Nina's house that explored this mysterious word. What I found was that it was an Indian-inspired curry with some Iraqi flare. It's a traditional Baghdadi Jewish recipe from Kolkata, India, where my grandfather was from. I like to think of this recipe as a fusion between my Iraqi background and my Indian upbringing. The two cultures were put together in this dish and passed down through generations in my family. There is never a family event where chitanni is not served. We often eat it with a version of Creamy Avocado Ginger Salsa (page 133) and A Pot o' Rice (page 228).

This recipe is pretty hands-off and a true set-it-and-forget-it type of meal. You have to wait for it to braise in the oven (that's pretty much it), but it's SO worth it. Don't forget to save some extra to make the Chitanni, Provolone & Shishito Cheesesteak (page 195)!

1. Preheat your oven to 300°F.

2. Pat the beef dry with paper towels and season on all sides with salt and black pepper. Leave your beef at room temperature while you prep all your other ingredients.

3. Mince the onions and ginger and thinly slice the garlic.

4. In a large Dutch oven or deep pot, heat the oil over medium-high heat until glistening. Working in batches to avoid crowding the pot, char your meat until dark brown on all sides, 10 to 15 minutes. Add more oil between batches if the pot is dry. Transfer the batches to a bowl as you work.

AUNTIE NINA'S SPICY SLOW-BRAISED BEEF CHITANNI
continued

Serve this with a big dollop of Creamy Avocado Ginger Salsa (page 133).

5. Turn off the heat, and add your onions to the pan drippings, and cook in the residual heat, 1 to 2 minutes. Turn the heat to medium, stirring constantly. You want to see a tad of golden browning on the onions, but not burnt or dark brown, 3 to 5 minutes. Add more oil as needed if the pot is dry.

6. Add the cayenne, garam masala, curry powder, cumin, turmeric powder, and salt and black pepper, giving it a nice toss with the onions and letting it all combine for another minute. Add your tomato paste, ginger, garlic, and tamarind paste, tossing periodically, until your tomato paste has darkened in color from a bright red to a darkened red wine, auburn hue, 1 to 2 minutes.

7. Return the beef to the pot, discarding any liquid that has formed in the bowl. Mix well and season with ½ teaspoon salt. Reduce the heat to medium, add the water, and scrape the browned bits from the bottom of the pot. Cook until the water has nearly all evaporated, 3 to 4 minutes. It's okay that the mixture looks thick or dry. The beef will give off lots of flavorful juices as it braises.

8. Cover the Dutch oven, transfer to the oven, and cook until the beef flakes off and shreds easily with a fork, 3 to 4 hours, stirring every hour or so. Your chitanni should not be watery or have too much liquid.

9. Serve the chitanni over white rice, spooning over all your oniony sauce. Finish with freshly chopped cilantro.

SERVES 2
30 MINUTES

CHITANNI, PROVOLONE & SHISHITO CHEESESTEAK

Two 6-inch hoagie rolls, split lengthwise

4 shishito peppers

1 tablespoon extra-virgin olive oil

1 cup shredded Auntie Nina's Spicy Slow-Braised Beef Chitanni (page 191), any extra fat or silver skins removed

2 slices provolone cheese

Hear me out: Take any extra chitanni (slow-braised beef) and make these sandwiches. Inspired by a classic cheesesteak, and the one from Matu in Los Angeles, these cheesesteaks use braised chitanni with melted provolone cheese and blistered shishito peppers. Shishito peppers are generally not that hot (but you may get one or two that are), and they add a nice brightening element to this cheesesteak, all rounded out on a warmed, toasted roll.

1. In a large dry cast-iron skillet with a lid or griddle set over medium heat, toast the interior of your hoagie rolls. Do this in batches if needed, 3 to 4 minutes. Set aside.

2. Add the shishito peppers and olive oil to the skillet over medium heat and cook, tossing often, until charred and soft, 4 to 6 minutes. Set aside.

3. Add the chitanni to the skillet and use a spatula to separate the beef into two piles each about the size of a hoagie roll. Warm through gently over medium-low heat for 2 to 3 minutes. You don't want to develop any crust or further browning, just warm through.

4. Increase the heat to medium and drape the provolone cheese over the meat. Cover with a lid to steam and melt your cheese completely, 1 to 2 minutes.

5. Using a spatula, transfer the beef and melted provolone cheese to your toasted rolls. Top with the shishito peppers. Close your hoagie roll and serve.

SERVES 4
ABOUT 3 HOURS 15 MINUTES

COFFEE & CAYENNE RUBBED RIBS WITH MUSTARD BARBECUE SAUCE

COFFEE & CAYENNE RUBBED RIBS

1 tablespoon black peppercorns

1½ teaspoons mustard seeds

¼ cup packed dark brown sugar

2 tablespoons ground medium-roast coffee, preferably freshly ground

¾ teaspoon cayenne pepper

1 tablespoon smoked paprika

1 tablespoon Diamond Crystal kosher salt

1 large rack pork baby back ribs (about 3 pounds), membrane removed (see note)

1 tablespoon yellow mustard

MUSTARD BARBECUE SAUCE

⅓ cup yellow mustard

2 tablespoons apple cider vinegar

2 tablespoons brown sugar

1 tablespoon Worcestershire or low-sodium soy sauce

¼ teaspoon cayenne pepper

Kosher salt and freshly ground black pepper

Set the ribs on your work surface meaty-side down. Using a sharp paring knife, place the tip of the blade underneath the membrane, wiggling it under, then use your fingers to pull off the membrane. You can also ask your butcher to do this for you!

These slow-roasted coffee and cayenne rubbed baby back pork ribs are fall-off-the-bone tender with a flavorful, smoky rub, and can't be any easier to make. Just wrap them up and place them in the oven to cook. When they're done, dip them in a quick (I promise, it's so easy) mustard barbecue sauce, inspired by the flavors of Carolina BBQ sauce. Serve with some pickles and coleslaw, and you are in for a feast.

1. **Make your Coffee & Cayenne Rub:** In a small, dry saucepan, toast your peppercorns and mustard seeds over medium heat until fragrant, 1 to 2 minutes. Transfer to a mortar and pestle or spice grinder to grind to a coarse powder. Add your brown sugar, coffee, cayenne, paprika, and salt and mix to combine. (Reserve the saucepan to make the Mustard Barbecue Sauce.)

2. **Prepare your ribs:** Line a sheet pan with parchment paper. Set your ribs on the pan, dry well with paper towels, and brush all sides with the mustard. Generously spread your rub mixture all around your ribs. Let your ribs sit at room temperature while the oven preheats. (You can also refrigerate them, uncovered, for 1 hour, or overnight.)

3. **Bake your ribs:** Position racks in the middle and upper third of the oven and preheat the oven to 250°F.

4. Arrange your ribs meaty-side up on the pan and seal tightly with aluminum foil. Transfer to the middle rack in the oven and bake until the ribs are fall-off-the-bone tender, about 3 hours.

5. **Make your Mustard Barbecue Sauce:** In the medium saucepan, mix the mustard, vinegar, brown sugar, Worcestershire, cayenne, and salt and black pepper to taste. Cook over medium heat and allow your sugar to melt and your sauce to thicken and turn a darker yellow, 4 to 5 minutes. You want the texture to be pourable and not too thick. Set aside until ready to serve. The sauce will firm up as it sits.

6. Remove the ribs from the oven. Increase the temperature to 450°F.

7. Carefully open your foil. Return the ribs to the top rack of the oven, and cook for another 5 minutes. Remove from the oven and let the ribs rest for 5 minutes. Transfer to a cutting board and cut the rack into individual ribs.

8. **To assemble:** Serve with the mustard barbecue sauce and your choice of sides.

SERVES 4
1 HOUR

GALBI-INSPIRED STEAK WITH QUICK PEAR KIMCHI

1 large Asian pear
(1 to 1½ pounds), peeled

GALBI-INSPIRED STEAK

¼ cup low-sodium soy sauce

2 tablespoons dark brown sugar

1-inch piece fresh ginger, grated

1 tablespoon toasted sesame oil

1 large garlic clove, grated

Freshly ground black pepper

1 pound steak, such as bavette, hanger, New York, rib-eye, or boneless short rib

QUICK PEAR KIMCHI

3 scallions

2 tablespoons rice vinegar

2 teaspoons gochugaru flakes

1 teaspoon toasted sesame oil

1 teaspoon toasted sesame seeds

Kosher salt

FOR SERVING

Toasted sesame seeds

Cooked white rice

Ssamjang

Butter lettuce or little gem lettuce leaves

Flaky salt

Toasted sesame oil

Gluten-free option: Swap in coconut aminos or tamari for the soy sauce.

If I'm going to Korean BBQ, I will never opt out of the galbi, Korean short ribs with a sweet and savory marinade made with pears, mirin, and sugar. This is inspired by that classic K-BBQ experience, paired with a sweet and spicy quick pear kimchi.

I love to serve this wrapped in lettuce cups, a style of a Korean dish known as *ssam*, meaning "wrapped." I also like to include fluffy white rice and ssamjang, a deeply flavorful Korean fermented soybean and chile paste. Here you'll make a lettuce pocket with rice, steak, kimchi, and ssamjang, served with a small dish of toasted sesame oil with flaky salt for even more dipping. Additional banchan (small side dishes served with a Korean meal) can be added, such as cucumber salad, potato salad, kimchi (like this pear kimchi), radishes, or bean sprouts.

Start cooking your rice before you begin prep (if you're not marinating your steak) so that you're ready to eat everything together by the time the rice is ready!

1. Coarsely grate ¼ cup of the Asian pear for the marinade. Set aside the rest for the kimchi.

2. **Marinate your steak:** In a large bowl, combine the grated pear, soy sauce, brown sugar, ginger, sesame oil, garlic, and black pepper to taste. Toss with your steak either in the large bowl directly or in a plastic bag, coating well. Cover and marinate at room temperature for 15 to 30 minutes, or refrigerate overnight.

3. **Make your Quick Pear Kimchi:** While the steak marinates, cut the remaining Asian pear into ½-inch cubes. Halve your scallions lengthwise and then cut crosswise into 2-inch lengths.

4. In a resealable container, combine the pear, scallions, vinegar, gochugaru, sesame oil, sesame seeds, and salt to taste. Cover and refrigerate for at least 15 minutes, until ready to serve, or up to overnight. The kimchi should turn a nice dark red once all the juices and liquid release.

continued...

GALBI-INSPIRED STEAK WITH QUICK PEAR KIMCHI
continued

5. When ready to cook your steak, place a wire rack in a sheet pan lined with parchment paper. Preheat your grill to high (or preheat a medium cast-iron skillet over high heat). Remove your steak from the marinade, scraping off any excess. Grill (or pan-fry) your steak, turning once, to an internal temperature of 125° to 130°F for medium-rare, 4 to 5 minutes per side, depending on the thickness of your steak. I like to get a lot of char on the outside of the steak (and the brown sugar will help make this char faster!) while still having a medium-rare center.

6. Transfer the steak to the wire rack to rest for at least 10 minutes. Transfer to a cutting board and thinly slice against the grain.

7. To serve: Top the sliced steak with a pinch of sesame seeds. Serve with the pear kimchi, rice, ssamjang, and lettuce to make wraps. In a small bowl, stir together some flaky salt and toasted sesame oil for dipping your steak before adding to the wrap.

SERVES 4
1 HOUR

BLACK PEPPER & CORIANDER RACK OF LAMB WITH MINT ZHOUG & CHICKPEAS

LAMB & CHICKPEAS

One 8-rib rack or two 4-rib small racks of lamb (1½ to 2 pounds total), trimmed and frenched (frenching optional)

1 tablespoon extra-virgin olive oil

1 tablespoon coarsely ground black pepper

1½ teaspoons ground coriander

Kosher salt

One 15-ounce can chickpeas, drained and rinsed

MINT ZHOUG

1 cup fresh mint leaves

2 large jalapeño chiles, roughly chopped (seeded if you want it less spicy!)

2 large garlic cloves, peeled but whole

½ teaspoon ground coriander

Kosher salt and freshly ground black pepper

2 tablespoons extra-virgin olive oil

Juice of 1 small lemon

continued...

I could probably eat lamb chops every night for dinner and be quite a happy camper. It may seem intimidating, but I promise that preparing a rack of lamb is really easy, and it cooks super quickly. All it takes is a high sear and then a fast finish in the oven. For this we're adding chickpeas with the lamb (hi, one pan), which turn soft and crunchy, working in tandem with the tender lamb chops.

The lamb is served with a quick zhoug, a traditional Yemenite condiment made with chiles and cilantro, but here I'm using mint. Serve the lamb and chickpeas with a generous pour of the spicy zhoug.

1. **Equipment:** Bring out your food processor or stand blender.

2. Preheat your oven to 400°F.

3. **Prep your Lamb & Chickpeas:** Pat your rack of lamb dry with paper towels. Transfer to a platter or cutting board and drizzle the olive oil all over the lamb. Then rub all sides of the lamb rack(s) evenly with the coarse black pepper, coriander, and salt, rubbing to ensure the seasoning is throughout all parts of the lamb. Let your lamb sit at room temperature. Pat your chickpeas dry and set aside.

4. **Make your Mint Zhoug:** In the food processor or blender, pulse the mint, jalapeños, garlic, coriander, and salt and black pepper to taste to make a thick paste. It should be chunky in texture and not too fine. Add your olive oil and lemon juice, pulsing again until combined and saucy. Season with more salt to taste. Transfer to a bowl or deli container, covered, and refrigerate until ready to serve.

5. **Cook your lamb:** Heat a large cast-iron or other ovenproof skillet over high heat. Carefully place the seasoned rack of lamb in the pan, fat-side down. Sear the rack of lamb on all sides until the lamb develops a nice browned crust, 10 to 12 minutes. You can use tongs to press the rack down on the pan to ensure that the crust is forming.

6. Pour the chickpeas all around the lamb. Do a quick toss in the skillet as best as you can to coat the chickpeas with any lamb fat in the pan. Turn the lamb rack so the fat side is facing up and transfer the skillet to the oven.

BLACK PEPPER & CORIANDER RACK OF LAMB WITH MINT ZHOUG & CHICKPEAS
continued

7. Roast to the desired temperature, preferably 125° to 130°F for medium rare. For a large rack, timing will be 18 to 24 minutes, for two smaller racks, 15 to 18 minutes.

8. Remove the lamb and chickpeas from the oven and transfer your lamb rack to a cutting board to rest for at least 10 minutes before slicing. Season the chickpeas in the skillet to taste with salt.

9. Slice the rack of lamb into individual chops, using the lamb bones to guide you to evenly cut between the chops.

10: To serve: Arrange the chickpeas on a platter and set your lamb chops on top. Finish with a heaping drizzling of mint zhoug.

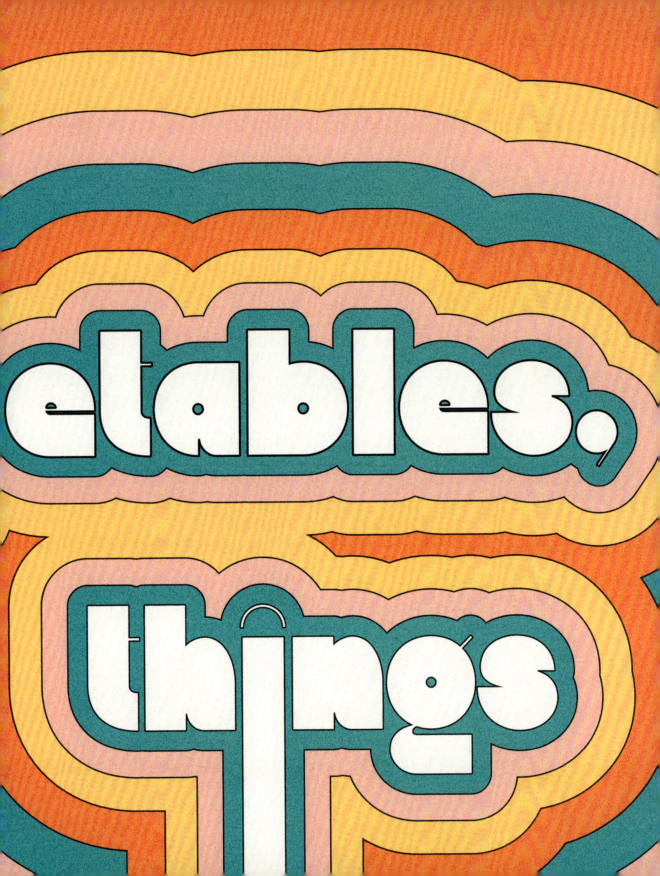

SERVES 4
30 MINUTES

MAPLE CHILI GLAZED CARROTS WITH CARROT-TOP SALSA VERDE

MAPLE CHILI GLAZED CARROTS

2 pounds carrots (8 to 12 medium carrots), peeled

¼ cup pure maple syrup

1 tablespoon chili powder

Kosher salt

CARROT-TOP SALSA VERDE

¼ cup finely chopped leafy carrot tops

¼ cup finely chopped fresh flat-leaf parsley

¼ cup extra-virgin olive oil

2 large garlic cloves, minced

2 tablespoons red wine vinegar

Kosher salt

Whenever this is on the table, it's always a surprising standout. Maple and chili powder together give you a little bit of sweet heat with a salty kick. Toss in carrots and roast until tender and you have a match made in heaven. Keep the carrot tops to make a zingy, red wine vinegar salsa verde that balances out the maple's sweetness and spice from the chili powder.

1. Preheat your oven to 400°F. Line a sheet pan or baking dish with parchment paper.

2. **Cut the carrots:** Cut the carrots on a bias into thirds, or so that each piece is about 3 inches long and no more than ½ inch wide. If the carrots have thick tops, cut them in half lengthwise.

3. Add the carrots to the sheet pan or baking dish. Mix with the maple syrup, chili powder, and salt (take care when seasoning, as most chili powders contain some salt), ensuring they are well coated. Arrange the carrots in a single layer.

4. Transfer to the oven and roast until the carrots are tender and caramelized, 20 to 25 minutes, turning them halfway through for even cooking.

5. **Make your Carrot-Top Salsa Verde:** In a medium bowl, combine the chopped carrot tops, parsley, olive oil, garlic, and vinegar. Mix well to incorporate. Season with salt to taste. Set aside until ready to serve.

6. **To serve:** Plate the roasted carrots on a serving platter and drizzle the carrot-top salsa verde over them.

SERVES 4
30 MINUTES

CHARRED CABBAGE WITH CALABRIAN CHILI BUTTER

1 medium head green cabbage (about 2 pounds)

2 tablespoons unsalted butter

2 teaspoons Calabrian chili paste

Kosher salt and freshly ground black pepper

Bacon Bread Crumbs (page 76)

¼ cup finely chopped fresh flat-leaf parsley

Lemon wedges, for squeezing

Vegetarian option and gluten-free option: Omit the bacon in the bread crumbs, or remove the bread crumbs altogether.

Cabbage is one of my favorite vegetables; grilled, roasted, raw, I am here for all forms of this crunchy veg. Here cabbage is charred and tossed with Calabrian chili paste and butter, and topped with crunchy Bacon Bread Crumbs (page 76) to create this smoky side dish. Chef's KISS!

1. Quarter your cabbage and cut out the core. Cut each cabbage quarter lengthwise into 1-inch-wide strips, then pull apart the layers.

2. In a large skillet or cast-iron pan, melt your butter over medium-high heat. Add your chili paste and mix to combine the two together.

3. Add your cabbage, season with salt and pepper, and use tongs to toss to combine. Cook undisturbed until deeply charred, 5 to 6 minutes. Toss once more and repeat until all the cabbage is slightly tender but still with a crunch, 5 to 6 minutes longer. Taste the cabbage and adjust with more salt and pepper if needed.

4. Pile high on a platter and finish with a heaping sprinkling of your bacon bread crumbs, parsley, and a squeeze of lemon juice.

SERVES 4
1 HOUR

SHAWARMA-SPICED WHOLE ROASTED CAULIFLOWER WITH GARLICKY TAHINI & QUICK-PICKLED ONIONS

If you ask me what you should make for a vegetarian main, I will most likely suggest this whole roasted cauliflower. It's hard for me to find more vegetarian-forward main dishes that leave me satisfied, but this one really delivers. Garlicky tahini is drizzled over soft and tender shawarma-spiced roasted cauliflower, then rounded out with crunchy quick-pickled dilly onions. It has the heat from the shawarma spice, the cooling effect from the tahini, and the crunch from the onions—quite literally an all-in-one meal. Trust me, you will be comin' back for seconds (and thirds).

SHAWARMA-SPICED CAULIFLOWER

2 small heads cauliflower (1½ to 2 pounds each)

1 teaspoon ground cumin

1 teaspoon ground coriander

1 teaspoon smoked paprika

1 teaspoon ground turmeric

1 teaspoon Diamond Crystal kosher salt

1 teaspoon freshly ground black pepper

½ teaspoon ground cinnamon

½ teaspoon cayenne pepper

½ cup extra-virgin olive oil

GARLICKY TAHINI

¼ cup well-stirred tahini (see note)

2 large garlic cloves, minced or grated

Juice of ½ large lemon

2 tablespoons cold water or 2 to 3 ice cubes

Kosher salt and freshly ground black pepper

1. Preheat your oven to 400°F. Line a sheet pan with parchment paper.

2. **Make the Shawarma-Spiced Cauliflower:** Cut away the green leaves and stem from the cauliflower, leaving the core intact. In a steamer basket or a wide deep pot, bring a few inches of water to a boil. Add your cauliflower and steam over medium-high heat until the cauliflower is crisp-tender, 8 to 10 minutes. You should be able to easily pierce it with the tip of a paring knife.

3. **Make the shawarma spice rub:** Meanwhile, in a large bowl, combine the cumin, coriander, paprika, turmeric, salt, black pepper, cinnamon, and cayenne. Mix well, then stir in the olive oil.

4. One at a time, use tongs to carefully transfer each steamed head of cauliflower to the bowl of spice rub. Let sit to cool for 5 minutes, then turn to coat all sides. Transfer the cauliflower to the lined sheet pan. Spoon the rest of the spice rub over both. (Hold onto the spice rub bowl for making the pickles.)

5. Transfer to the oven and roast until the cauliflower is completely tender and a golden crust forms on the outside, 30 to 40 minutes. You can test this by placing a fork into the cauliflower—if it goes in easily, it is tender and ready!

6. **Prepare the Garlicky Tahini:** While your cauliflower is in the oven, in a small bowl, whisk together the tahini, garlic, lemon juice, cold water or ice cubes, and pinch of each of salt and black pepper. Stir well to combine,

continued...

SHAWARMA-SPICED WHOLE ROASTED CAULIFLOWER WITH GARLICKY TAHINI & QUICK-PICKLED ONIONS
continued

QUICK-PICKLED ONIONS

½ small red onion, thinly sliced

1 tablespoon extra-virgin olive oil

½ teaspoon toasted sesame seeds, plus more for sprinkling

Juice of ½ large lemon

¼ cup roughly torn fresh dill

Kosher salt

Tahini is a paste made from sesame seeds; it's used in a lot of Middle Eastern cooking.

Serve with Za'atar-Roasted Kabocha Squash with Pomegranate Dressing (page 226).

then stir occasionally while the cauliflower continues to roast. As the ice melts (if you used it), you'll get a thick, smooth, and creamy sauce. If the mixture is too thick and pasty, add more ice or water as needed.

7. **Make your Quick-Pickled Onions:** In the bowl used for the spice rub, combine the red onion, olive oil, sesame seeds, lemon juice, dill, and salt to taste. Toss to combine and let sit until serving time.

8. **To serve:** Once the cauliflower is done, transfer it to a serving platter. Drizzle the garlic tahini over the cauliflower, allowing it to seep into the crevices. Reserve any extra sauce for serving alongside the cauliflower. Sprinkle your cauliflower with toasted sesame seeds and your quick-pickled onions. Serve the cauliflower whole, or slice it into wedges.

SERVES 4
45 MINUTES

PAN-FRIED PANKO-CRUSTED EGGPLANT WITH JAMMY CHERRY TOMATOES & BURRATA

2 medium eggplants, sliced into ½-inch rounds

Kosher salt

¼ cup extra-virgin olive oil

2 large garlic cloves, thinly sliced

Freshly ground black pepper

¼ teaspoon red pepper flakes (optional)

2 cups cherry tomatoes

2 large eggs

1½ cups panko bread crumbs

⅓ cup grated Parmigiano-Reggiano cheese

Neutral oil, for shallow-frying

8 ounces fresh burrata cheese

10 fresh basil leaves, chiffonade-cut, for garnish

continued...

Recently I've been loving eggplant Parmesan, and this is sort of a deconstructed version. Instead of a casserole dish in the oven, this includes panko-crusted fried eggplant, which is then topped with jammy cherry tomatoes and tons of basil. No need to turn the oven on here! The sweet cherry tomatoes complement the fried eggplant beautifully, all rounded out with creamy burrata and fresh basil.

1. **Prepare your eggplant:** Line a tray with paper towels and set the eggplant rounds on the paper towels. Sprinkle the tops with salt and allow them to sit for 15 minutes to release excess moisture.

2. **Make the jammy cherry tomatoes:** Meanwhile, in a large skillet, heat the olive oil over medium heat until it shimmers. Add your garlic and sauté for 1 to 2 minutes until fragrant, making sure the garlic doesn't burn (you want your garlic to soften but not bring on any color). Season with salt, black pepper, and a pinch of red pepper flakes (if using). Toss to combine with your garlic.

3. Add the cherry tomatoes and cook, stirring occasionally, until they start to blister and lightly burst, 5 to 6 minutes. I like to take them off the heat when they are all not fully burst, since I want some whole cherry tomatoes and not a tomato sauce. You can give them a little pop with the back of your spatula if they aren't releasing any moisture or liquid. Season to taste with salt and black pepper. Remove from the heat and set aside until ready to assemble.

4. **Fry your eggplant:** Set up a dredging station in two shallow bowls. In one bowl, whisk your eggs and season with salt and black pepper. In the second bowl, mix together the panko, Parmesan, and salt and black pepper to taste.

5. Line a plate with paper towels and have near the stove. Pour ½ inch of oil into a medium skillet and heat over medium-high heat until hot, about 350°F.

6. Dry each eggplant slice the best you can with a paper towel and then dip each slice first in the beaten eggs, then in the panko/Parmesan mixture, making sure the tops and bottoms of the slices are fully coated.

SIDES, VEGETABLES & THINGS

PAN-FRIED PANKO-CRUSTED EGGPLANT WITH JAMMY CHERRY TOMATOES & BURRATA
continued

7. Working in batches to avoid crowding, add the coated eggplant slices to the skillet and fry, turning once, until golden brown and crispy, 1 to 2 minutes per side. Transfer to the paper towels to drain excess oil. Season with a dash of salt.

8. **To serve:** Arrange the eggplant on a serving platter. Tear the burrata cheese into bite-size pieces and set on top of the eggplant. Spoon the jammy cherry tomatoes over the eggplant and burrata, making sure to get all of that garlicky oil over everything. Garnish with your sliced basil. I like to finish the whole dish with a big crank of black pepper.

SHEET PAN SALT & PEPPER RADISHES

SERVES 4
30 MINUTES

1 pound assorted radishes, greens removed

1 tablespoon extra-virgin olive oil

Kosher salt and freshly ground black pepper

1 tablespoon unsalted butter

Lemon wedges, for serving

Flaky salt, for serving

Vegan option and dairy-free option: Omit the butter or swap in vegan butter.

Radishes don't get the love they deserve and if you've never had them roasted, you're missing out! Similar to a roasted potato but with a hint of sweetness and bite, this will be a nice addition to any lunch or dinner. Salt, pepper, lemon, and butter are all you need to elevate this spicy vegetable. Use any radish options available, such as watermelon radish, daikon radish, or red radish.

1. Position a rack in the bottom third of the oven and preheat the oven to 400°F. Line a sheet pan with parchment paper.

2. Wash and dry the radishes. Cut your radishes through the stem into roughly ½-inch pieces. (If you have some radishes on the smaller side, you can halve them.)

3. Add your radishes to the lined pan and drizzle with the olive oil. Season with salt and pepper, tossing to coat. Arrange all the radishes cut-side down.

4. Transfer to the oven and roast until the radishes are tender but with a bite to them (not soft or mushy!) and browned on the cut sides, 25 to 30 minutes. No need to flip.

5. Right out of the oven, add your butter and toss with the radishes to melt. Transfer to a serving plate and finish with a fresh squeeze of lemon and flaky salt.

SERVES 4
30 MINUTES

CHILI GARLIC BRUSSELS SPROUTS WITH FURIKAKE

1 pound brussels sprouts, trimmed and halved lengthwise

2 tablespoons extra-virgin olive oil

Freshly ground black pepper

2 tablespoons chili garlic sauce, such as sambal oelek

2 tablespoons low-sodium soy sauce

1 tablespoon honey

1 tablespoon furikake, plus more for serving

Gluten-free option: Swap in coconut aminos or tamari for the soy sauce.

When I brought these brussels sprouts to our family's Thanksgiving potluck, my cousin, Jessica, said this was the only item on the table that her kids would eat. These have sambal oelek, a tangy, punchy, and zippy condiment I always have on hand. It works especially well with these crispy, crunchy brussels sprouts. These sprouts are simply roasted in the oven, then tossed with a sticky, spicy sambal sauce and finished with furikake, a Japanese seasoning oftentimes made of toasted sesame seeds, chili, bonito flakes, nori, salt, and sugar.

1. **Roast your brussels sprouts:** Position a rack in the bottom third of the oven and preheat the oven to 425°F. Line a sheet pan with parchment paper.

2. On the lined pan, combine the brussels sprouts, olive oil, and black pepper. Toss to coat. Arrange the sprouts cut-side down.

3. Transfer to the oven and roast until deeply golden brown and fork-tender (but each sprout should also still have a little bite to it—we don't want them mushy!), about 20 minutes.

4. **Make your sauce:** While the sprouts are roasting, in a medium skillet, combine the chili garlic sauce, soy sauce, honey, and black pepper to taste. Bring to a simmer over medium heat, mixing periodically until a thick glaze forms, 1 to 2 minutes. You know it's good to go when you can draw a clean line through the glaze with your spatula. Remove from the heat until ready to toss.

5. Transfer your roasted brussels sprouts to the skillet and bring the heat back to medium-low. Toss with your sauce until completely coated and glossy. Turn off the heat and add your furikake. Toss once more, transfer to a serving dish, and top with even more furikake.

SOUR CREAM & CARAMELIZED ONION POTATOES

SERVES 4
45 MINUTES

1½ pounds small baby potatoes

Kosher salt

2 tablespoons unsalted butter

1 large yellow onion, minced

Freshly ground black pepper

¼ cup full-fat sour cream

1 tablespoon distilled white vinegar, plus more for serving

¼ cup finely chopped fresh chives

One of the very first recipes I posted on my blog in 2012 was a caramelized onion potato salad. I had just learned how to caramelize onions, so naturally, I put them in everything. This is an updated version, which gives big pierogi energy. The onions are tossed with fork-tender baby potatoes and then topped with chopped chives, for double the alliums. The potatoes are then placed over a vinegared sour cream. (Add even more vinegar before serving!)

This will be a tangy, pillowy side dish you'll make on repeat.

1. Boil the potatoes: Place the potatoes in a large pot with enough water to cover the potatoes by about 1 inch. Bring to a boil and add a few big pinches of salt. Reduce the heat and simmer until the potatoes are fork-tender, 10 to 15 minutes. Timing may vary depending on the size of your potatoes. Drain and return to the pot with the heat off. You want to keep them warm.

2. Caramelize your onions: Meanwhile, in a medium skillet, melt 1 tablespoon of the butter over medium heat. Add the onion and cook, stirring often and adjusting the heat as necessary to keep it from burning, until totally soft and deeply golden brown. This should take 25 to 30 minutes. Season the caramelized onion with salt and black pepper.

3. While your potatoes and onion are cooking, in a small bowl, mix together the sour cream, vinegar, and salt to taste. Set aside until ready to serve.

4. To the warm potatoes, add the caramelized onions, half of the chives, and the remaining 1 tablespoon butter. Toss until the butter is totally melted. Season to taste with salt and black pepper.

5. To serve: Spoon the sour cream mixture onto a platter and spread it into an even layer. Top with your potatoes and garnish with the remaining chives and black pepper. Drizzle a little more vinegar over the potatoes if preferred (I like to!).

You can opt to swap out the sour cream here for Horseradish Cream (page 93) for an extra spicy kick and serve alongside Beet Soup (page 93).

SERVES 4
30 MINUTES

ROASTED BROCCOLINI WITH CILANTRO-LIME VINAIGRETTE

Broccolini, the more sophisticated, milder, and sweeter version of broccoli, is roasted simply with salt, pepper, and olive oil. Once roasted but still vibrant green, I drizzle it with a tangy cilantro lime vinaigrette that creates a pungent, peppery flavor that will liven up any main.

ROASTED BROCCOLINI

2 large bunches of broccolini (about 2 pounds)

2 tablespoons extra-virgin olive oil

Kosher salt and freshly ground black pepper

CILANTRO-LIME VINAIGRETTE

¼ cup packed fresh cilantro

2 tablespoons extra-virgin olive oil

1 small garlic clove, peeled but whole

2 tablespoons cold water

1 tablespoon fresh lime juice (about ½ lime)

Kosher salt and freshly ground black pepper

The vinaigrette can be used in other recipes. Try it poured over Spiced Lamb Meatballs (page 178) or Really Good Roast Chicken (page 155).

1. **Equipment:** Bring out your stand blender.

2. **Roast your Broccolini:** Preheat your oven to 400°F. Line a sheet pan with parchment paper.

3. Trim off about 2 inches from the stems of your broccolini. If the stalks of your broccolini are a tad large, you can halve them lengthwise. Set your broccolini on the sheet pan and drizzle with the olive oil. Season with salt and black pepper.

4. Transfer to the oven and roast until the florets have brightened in color with a little char, and the broccolini has softened with a nice bite to it, 20 to 25 minutes, tossing halfway through.

5. **Make your Cilantro-Lime Vinaigrette:** While the broccolini is roasting, in a blender, combine your cilantro, olive oil, garlic, water, lime juice, salt and pepper. Blend until completely smooth; it should be a nice dressing consistency, not too thick, and completely emulsified. Adjust with salt and pepper to taste.

6. **To serve:** Transfer the roasted broccolini to a serving plate and drizzle with your vinaigrette.

PECORINO PAPRIKA POLENTA FRIES

SERVES 4
2 HOURS

4 cups water

1 cup coarsely ground yellow cornmeal

Kosher salt and freshly ground black pepper

¼ cup grated Pecorino Romano cheese, plus more for serving

2 tablespoons extra-virgin olive oil

½ teaspoon smoked paprika

Polenta, or boiled cornmeal, is often served with dishes like braised short ribs, or for a hearty breakfast. But it can also be transformed into polenta fries. After being sliced into batons and baked in the oven, the polenta fries become soft inside and crunchy on the outside. I like to top them with paprika and loads of Pecorino Romano cheese for saltiness and a kick of spice.

1. Line a half-sheet pan (18 by 13-inch) with parchment paper.

2. In a medium saucepan, bring the water to a boil over high heat. Once boiling, gradually whisk in your cornmeal, stirring constantly to ensure no clumps or lumps. Allow your polenta to form bubbles and boil for 1 to 2 minutes, continuing to stir. Season with salt and black pepper.

3. Reduce the heat to low and cook, whisking constantly until the polenta has thickened enough that you can see the trail your whisk makes as you stir, 5 to 7 minutes. Turn off the heat and add your cheese and continue whisking until it melts. Taste and adjust seasonings with more salt and pepper.

4. Scrape the cooked polenta onto the lined pan, spreading evenly with an offset spatula so that the polenta fills the pan with an even, ½-inch-thick layer. Refrigerate, uncovered, until firm, about 1 hour, or covered with plastic wrap for up to 1 day.

5. Place two racks in the center area of the oven. Preheat your oven to 425°F. Line two sheet pans with parchment paper.

6. Flip the polenta onto a cutting board and remove the parchment. Cut the polenta lengthwise into thirds, then cut crosswise into 14 to 15 strips, yielding 42 to 45 fries, about ¼ inch wide, and 4½ inches long.

7. Carefully divide the fries between the two sheet pans, spreading them in an even layer. Drizzle with the olive oil. Use your hands to gently coat the top of the fries. There is no need to flip and oil the other side, and the fries will get naturally oily and crispy on the bottom side.

8. Place the sheet pans on two different racks toward the middle of the oven. Bake until the fries are completely golden brown and crispy throughout, 30 to 35 minutes, gently flipping the fries and swapping the placement of the pans halfway through the baking time.

9. Carefully transfer the fries to a serving platter. (I like to line it with some brown parchment!) Top with shredded Pecorino Romano cheese, the smoked paprika, and a crank of pepper.

This pairs beautifully with Very Shallot-y Mayo (page 63) or Sambal Aioli (page 55) for all your dipping desires.

SERVES 4
45 MINUTES

ZA'ATAR-ROASTED KABOCHA SQUASH WITH POMEGRANATE DRESSING

ZA'ATAR-ROASTED KABOCHA SQUASH

1 medium kabocha squash (about 2 pounds)

¼ cup extra-virgin olive oil

2 teaspoons za'atar, plus more for serving

Kosher salt and freshly ground black pepper

POMEGRANATE DRESSING

1 tablespoon pomegranate molasses

1 tablespoon fresh lemon juice

1 tablespoon Dijon mustard

Kosher salt and freshly ground black pepper

¼ cup extra-virgin olive oil

Pomegranate arils, for serving

If you've made the Pomegranate Yogurt Marinated Grilled Chicken (page 174), then you know that pomegranate molasses has a pungent, tangy flavor. It works really well with za'atar, too, a Middle Eastern spice blend of herbs, sumac, and sesame seeds. Here za'atar is tossed together with kabocha squash (and, yes, you can eat the skin!), which is sweeter than other squash, similar in flavor and texture to sweet potato and pumpkin. The squash is then roasted and served with a quick pomegranate dressing, and some crunch from fresh arils, too.

While this is using kabocha squash, you can also try this recipe with any kind of squash, like acorn or delicata. Optional to serve with a swoosh of ricotta, labneh, or yogurt, too.

1. **Roast your squash:** Position a rack in the bottom third of the oven and preheat your oven to 400°F. Line a sheet pan with parchment paper.

2. Scrub and halve your kabocha squash lengthwise through the stem. Remove the seeds with a spoon, and cut the squash into 1-inch-thick wedges. Transfer the squash to the lined sheet pan and add the olive oil, the za'atar, and salt and black pepper. (When seasoning, keep in mind that some za'atar blends already have salt in them.) Mix until the squash is completely coated with the seasoning mixture, then arrange in an even layer.

3. Transfer to the oven and roast, without flipping, until fork-tender and caramelized, about 30 minutes.

4. **Make your Pomegranate Dressing:** While your squash is roasting, in a medium bowl, whisk together the pomegranate molasses, lemon juice, mustard, and salt and black pepper to taste until combined. While whisking, slowly start streaming in your olive oil to completely emulsify your dressing. Taste and season with salt and pepper if needed.

5. **To serve:** Pile the squash on a platter, drizzle generously with your dressing, and sprinkle with pomegranate arils and za'atar.

SERVES 4
1 HOUR

1 cup basmati or jasmine rice

1½ cups cold water

1 tablespoon extra-virgin olive oil or unsalted butter

1 teaspoon Diamond Crystal kosher salt

A POT O' RICE

Almost every meal pairs well with white rice, so, of course, I have to include here how to make a really good pot of fluffy rice. It's taken me years to get the right pot of rice, one that's not too hard, or too mushy, and to be honest, it wasn't until quite recently that I got it down. If you're using basmati or jasmine, the key is soaking your rice. I love my rice cooker (my Zojirushi is one of my favorite gadgets), but mastering a pot of rice on the stovetop is a useful skill to learn.

1. In a medium saucepan or pot with a lid, add your rice and rinse 8 to 10 times until the water runs clear. Cover the saucepan or pot with a fresh batch of water and let your rice soak for 30 minutes.

2. After soaking, drain off the water and add 1½ cups fresh cold water, the olive oil, and salt. Toss to combine.

3. Bring this to a gentle simmer over medium-high heat, uncovered. As soon as it's bubbling (you don't want a rapid boil here), reduce the heat to low, cover, and set a timer for 15 minutes.

4. Remove from the heat and let your rice rest, covered, for 5 minutes. Uncover and fluff your rice to serve.

SERVES 4
10 MINUTES

2 tablespoons extra-virgin olive oil

1 cup fine couscous

Grated zest and juice of 1 large lemon

2 teaspoons Calabrian chili paste

Kosher salt and freshly ground black pepper

1 cup water

LEMONY COUSCOUS WITH A KICK

There are a number of dinner options in this book, and this couscous will pair with most of them. This is the grain that I love to make alongside my dinners. Couscous takes no time at all to cook—I'm talking less than 10 minutes. The "kick" here is Calabrian chili, which works nicely with the couscous, and loads of lemon juice and zest to boot.

1. In a medium pot with a lid, heat up your olive oil over medium-high heat until glistening. Add your couscous, lemon zest, Calabrian chili paste, and salt and black pepper. Toss to combine and toast, stirring constantly, until the couscous has taken on a nice light brown color (not burned!) and you smell a toasty aroma from the pot, 2 to 3 minutes.

2. Add the water and bring to a boil. Reduce the heat to low, cover, and cook until all the water has been absorbed, 2 to 3 minutes.

3. Remove from the heat, open the lid, and fluff with a fork. Add half of the lemon juice and toss to combine. Taste and add more lemon juice if needed.

SIDES, VEGETABLES & THINGS

MAKES ABOUT 24 COOKIES
1 HOUR 15 MINUTES

TAHINI CHOCOLATE CHIP COOKIES WITH TOASTED SESAME SEEDS

- 8 tablespoons (1 stick/ 4 ounces/115g) unsalted butter, sliced, at room temperature
- ½ cup (100g) packed dark brown sugar
- ½ cup (100g) granulated sugar
- ⅓ cup (100g) well-stirred tahini
- 2 teaspoons vanilla extract
- 1 large egg, at room temperature
- 1 teaspoon (3g) Diamond Crystal kosher salt
- ½ teaspoon (3g) baking soda
- 1½ cups (180g) all-purpose flour
- 4 ounces chocolate, plus 2 ounces (60% to 70% cacao), coarsely chopped
- Toasted sesame seeds and flaky salt, for topping

To get perfectly round cookies, after you add sesame seeds and salt, use a round cookie cutter or the rim of a drinking glass to ring and shape the cookies when they come out of the oven. Once they have cooled, they will retain their shape, so do this relatively quickly.

There is nothing better than biting into a warm chocolate chip cookie—except maybe when it also has a bit of tahini in it. Tahini adds moisture, texture, and savoriness, making this sweet treat just about as delicious as a cookie can get. The pairing also makes for a cookie rich in texture, with a soft chewy inside and crispy crackly edges. Top with sesame seeds and salt as they come out of the oven for extra nuttiness and crunch.

1. **Equipment:** Get out your stand mixer if using.

2. In a stand mixer fitted with the paddle (or in a large bowl with a spatula), combine your softened butter, brown sugar, and granulated sugar. Mix on medium speed until doughy and combined, 1 to 2 minutes.

3. Add your tahini, vanilla, and egg and mix for another minute or so until everything is incorporated. Add your kosher salt and baking soda, mixing until fully combined. Mix in your flour until just combined. Use a silicone spatula to gently fold in 4 ounces of the chocolate chunks.

4. Cover and refrigerate the cookie dough for at least 30 minutes. (But you can chill your dough for up to a day ahead!)

5. When ready to bake, position a rack in the center of the oven and preheat the oven to 325°F. Line a sheet pan with parchment paper.

6. Use a 1-ounce/2-tablespoon scoop or your hands to form 8 balls of chilled cookie dough (about the size of a Ping-Pong ball). Place them on the prepared sheet pan, leaving about 2 inches between the cookies. Refrigerate the remaining dough while you bake the first batch.

7. Using the remaining 2 ounces chocolate chunks, press onto the tops of the cookie dough balls.

8. Bake until the edges are pale golden brown and the centers are set but still slightly soft, 12 to 14 minutes. (Depending on how long you've chilled your dough, you may need to add a minute or so to the baking time.)

9. Remove the cookies from the oven and immediately finish with a sprinkling of toasted sesame seeds and flaky salt. Allow them to cool on the baking sheet for 10 to 15 minutes to help them set before transferring to a wire rack to cool completely.

10. Repeat with the remaining dough to make more batches of cookies, either waiting for the baking sheet to cool down or using a second baking sheet.

SERVES 6 TO 8
2 HOURS 15 MINUTES

BANANA BREAD

8 tablespoons (1 stick/ 4 ounces/115g) unsalted butter, at room temperature

½ cup (100g) granulated sugar

½ cup (100g) packed dark brown sugar

1½ cups (about 400g) mashed bananas (about 4 very ripe bananas)

½ cup (about 120g) whole-milk Greek yogurt or mascarpone

2 large eggs, at room temperature

2 teaspoons vanilla extract

1 tablespoon hojicha tea powder

1 teaspoon (5g) baking powder

1 teaspoon (6g) baking soda

½ teaspoon (1.5g) Diamond Crystal kosher salt

1½ cups (180g) all-purpose flour

HOJICHA GLAZE

1 cup powdered sugar, sifted

2 tablespoons whole milk, nondairy milk, or water

1 teaspoon hojicha tea powder

½ teaspoon (1.5g) Diamond Crystal kosher salt

BROWN SUGAR HOJICHA BANANA BREAD

Hojicha is a Japanese green tea that's been roasted over charcoal. It has a deeply nutty and almost smoky flavor with a little hint of sweet chocolate. In powder form, it's highly concentrated, and I just knew it would pair really well with bananas. Enter hojicha banana bread. The tea caramelizes with the bananas and the vanilla beautifully, so much so that my dad has said (many times) that this is the best banana bread he's ever had. I have to agree!

1. **Make the Banana Bread:** Preheat your oven to 325°F. Butter a 9 by 5-inch loaf pan. (I will just borrow a teaspoon or so of the butter from the batter.) Line the pan with a strip of parchment paper that hangs over the long edges so that the baked loaf is easier to remove.

2. In a large bowl, combine the softened butter, granulated sugar, and brown sugar and use a large spoon or flexible spatula to mash until completely combined.

3. Add your mashed bananas, yogurt, eggs, and vanilla and mix well until you have a smooth and wet batter. It is okay if there are some banana lumps here, but you shouldn't be seeing any white streaks from the yogurt.

4. Add your hojicha tea powder, baking powder, baking soda, and salt. Mix well until your batter is formed. Gently fold in your flour until just combined. Do not overmix.

5. Pour the batter into the prepared loaf pan, spreading it evenly. Lightly tap the pan against the counter to remove any bubbles.

6. Transfer to the oven and bake until a toothpick inserted into the center of the loaf comes out clean, 1 hour to 1 hour 10 minutes. You can also test doneness by inserting an instant-read thermometer; it should read 200° to 206°F.

7. Let the banana bread cool in the pan for about 10 minutes and then loosen gently from the sides of the pan. Using the parchment strip, lift the bread from the pan and carefully transfer onto a cooling rack to cool completely, 45 to 50 minutes.

8. **Make your Hojicha Glaze:** While your banana bread is cooling, in a medium bowl, whisk together the powdered sugar, milk, hojicha powder, and salt. Your glaze shouldn't be too runny or too thick, but a nice drizzle. Adjust with more milk if needed to reach your desired consistency.

9. Drizzle the glaze over the banana bread before slicing.

SERVES 3
45 MINUTES

RED WINE–POACHED PEARS WITH VANILLA YOGURT & PISTACHIOS

3 firm-ripe medium pears, preferably Bosc

1 cup red wine

¼ cup maple syrup, plus 1 tablespoon

2 tablespoons fresh lemon juice

2 teaspoons vanilla extract

1 cinnamon stick, or 1 teaspoon ground cinnamon

¼ teaspoon Diamond Crystal kosher salt

½ cup whole-milk Greek yogurt

¼ cup pistachios, minced to a coarse powder

Picture it: You're at a dinner party, and you've had appetizers, dinner, and now it's time for dessert. Then these poached pears arrive at the table, flavor-packed with cinnamon and wine, a tender pairing with crunchy pistachios and yogurt. I like to serve these on individual dessert plates for each guest. You can also swap the yogurt to serve this à la mode with some vanilla bean ice cream. The perfect way to end your perfect meal. I won't judge if you want to have this for breakfast!

1. Peel the pears, halve them lengthwise, and use a melon baller or small measuring spoon to remove the cores.

2. **Poach your pears:** In a medium skillet, combine the red wine, ¼ cup of the maple syrup, the lemon juice, 1 teaspoon of the vanilla, the cinnamon stick, and salt. Bring this mixture to a gentle simmer over medium heat, 2 to 3 minutes.

3. Reduce the heat to medium-low and add your pears cut-side up. Simmer until the pears are fork-tender and the color has turned a nice auburn from the wine, 15 to 20 minutes, flipping halfway through and basting any spots on the pears that may have not been submerged fully. You want your pears to poach low and slow so they get soft and infused.

4. Bring the heat up to high and cook until the syrup thickens enough to coat the back of a spoon, 2 to 3 minutes longer. We will use that for serving. Turn off the heat and cool slightly for 3 to 5 minutes.

5. **Make the vanilla yogurt:** While your pears are poaching, in a medium bowl, combine the yogurt and the remaining 1 tablespoon maple syrup and 1 teaspoon vanilla. Set aside.

6. **To assemble:** Slather a dollop of your yogurt in three shallow bowls, and top each with two poached pear halves, using tongs to shake off any excess liquid. Top with a dusting of pistachios and finish with a drizzle of the syrup from the skillet.

SALTED CARAMEL CHOCOLATE MOUSSE

SERVES 4
AT LEAST 4 HOURS 30 MINUTES

3 large eggs, at room temperature

1 tablespoon granulated sugar, plus 1 cup

2 ounces chocolate (60% to 70% cacao), finely chopped, plus 1 ounce shaved (I use a vegetable peeler)

½ cup room temperature heavy cream, plus 1 cup cold

8 tablespoons (1 stick/ 4 ounces) unsalted butter, cubed and cold

¾ teaspoon flaky salt, plus more for serving

Making homemade caramel might seem intimidating, but bear with me: All it takes are some simple techniques and patience! Inspired by my dad's favorite ice cream flavor from McConnell's Ice Cream, Salted Caramel Chip, this mousse is as simple as it is impressive. A mousse is something I love to prepare ahead for any dinner party and it will leave your guests thinking you worked harder than you actually did.

1. **Equipment:** Get out your stand mixer or electric mixer.

2. **Separate your yolks and egg whites:** Crack your egg in half, and place the egg over flat fingers, allowing the egg whites to separate between your fingers over a bowl, transferring your egg yolk to a separate small bowl. Repeat with the other eggs. Save the egg whites for an omelet or pavlova!

3. **Make your chocolate base:** Fill a medium pot with 1 to 2 inches of water (depending on the size of your pot). On top of the pot, add a heat-safe bowl that fits on top, creating a double boiler. The water should not be touching the bowl, so remove any water if this is the case. Bring this to a gentle simmer on medium heat and then reduce to low heat.

4. Add in your egg yolks and the 1 tablespoon granulated sugar. Whisk constantly until this mixture doubles in size, with slight bubbles forming, 2 to 3 minutes. Keep the heat low so you don't scramble the eggs.

5. Add 2 ounces of your chopped chocolate, whisking to melt, for 4 to 5 minutes. Be patient and allow time for the chocolate to completely melt as you continue to stir. Remove the bowl of melted chocolate from the heat and set it aside at room temperature. Discard the water from the medium pot, and set it back on the stovetop.

6. **Make your caramel:** Add the remaining 1 cup sugar to the medium pot and shake into an even layer. Set over medium heat, allowing the sugar to melt. Once it starts to melt and the sugar begins to dissolve, use a silicone spatula to scrape the sides of the pan so the sugar doesn't burn. If you are starting to see some burning, reduce the heat. Your sugar may look sandy or clumpy, but just keep waiting and stirring in places where there is smoke or burning until it becomes one melted mixture, and turns a nice amber color, 6 to 7 minutes.

7. Turn off the heat, and whisk in your cubed butter. At this point, it should bubble, this is normal. Keep mixing until the butter and sugar become one mixture.

continued...

SWEETS & TREATS

SALTED CARAMEL CHOCOLATE MOUSSE
continued

8. Add ½ cup of the heavy cream and whisk until combined. Finish with the flaky salt.

9. Measure out 2 tablespoons of the caramel and set aside in a small bowl for drizzling when serving. Transfer your remaining caramel to a medium bowl and let it come to room temperature. (If prepping a day ahead, store your caramel covered in the fridge, otherwise, just keep it at room temperature.)

10. Make your whipped cream: In your stand mixer or electric mixer, pour the remaining 1 cup heavy cream and whisk extremely well on high for 5 to 6 minutes until soft peaks form. If you are doing this by hand with a whisk, just keep whisking fast, and be patient, as this will take more time! The whipped cream should look shiny, and not dry.

11. Set aside half of your whipped cream covered in the fridge for serving, and gently fold in the remaining half whipped cream to the chocolate mixture, in 2 batches, making sure no streaks are there, and being careful not to overmix to ensure we keep the airy texture. Once completely combined, and your caramel is at room temperature, gently fold in your caramel until incorporated.

12. Transfer your mousse to 4 small cups or glasses and cover. Refrigerate for a minimum of 4 hours or overnight.

13. To serve: Remove your mousse from the fridge and top with your whipped cream, a drizzle of the reserved caramel, some flaky salt, and chocolate shavings. If your caramel has hardened, warm it in the microwave for 10 to 20 seconds or on the stovetop over low heat.

MAKES 2 LOAVES
7 HOURS (OR 1 DAY)

BROWN BUTTER & MISO CINNAMON BABKA

BABKA DOUGH

8 tablespoons (1 stick/ 4 ounces/115g) unsalted butter

½ cup (120g) whole milk

½ ounce (14g) active dry yeast

3½ cups (420g) all-purpose flour

¼ cup (50g) granulated sugar

¼ cup (50g) packed brown sugar

1 teaspoon (3g) Diamond Crystal kosher salt

2 large eggs, plus 1 egg yolk, at room temperature

BROWN BUTTER & MISO CINNAMON FILLING & SYRUP

8 tablespoons (1 stick/ 4 ounces/115g) unsalted butter

1 cup (200g) packed dark brown sugar

3 tablespoons white miso

2 teaspoons ground cinnamon

2 teaspoons vanilla extract

2 tablespoons Simple Syrup (page 250)

continued…

Babkas are a big deal in my family. This Jewish braided sweet brioche bread can be filled with a variety of options, but chocolate is most common. My Aunt Renne and Uncle Norman live on the East Coast and they always bring over babka from their family's bakery in New Jersey. Everyone goes nuts for it.

In honor of my family's obsession with babka, I'm going to take this popular family favorite in a new direction with a nutty brown butter and miso cinnamon filling. While this babka does not include chocolate (for your chocolate fix, see Tahini Chocolate Chip Cookies, page 232), it is just as rich in flavors. The brioche dough is fluffy and soft, and the cinnamon's sweet, earthy flavor makes the babka reminiscent of a cinnamon roll. Add some miso paste to complete this sweet bread and serve it warm. I guarantee you (and your family) won't be able to have just one bite.

1. **Equipment:** Bring out your stand mixer with the dough hook.

2. **Make the Babka Dough:** In a medium saucepan, melt the butter over medium heat. Once foamy, stir often, until the foam subsides, 4 to 5 minutes. The butter should be nice and golden and smelling nutty. If you see the butter getting too dark, then remove it from the heat. Transfer to a large bowl and set aside.

3. In the same pot off the heat, add the milk and let it warm until it reaches 110°F. This should take 1 to 2 minutes. Add your yeast, give it a stir, and let sit for about 5 minutes, until your yeast is foamy and bubbly. If you don't see any foaming or small bubbles forming, repeat this step with new yeast and milk to ensure your yeast is still alive!

4. In a stand mixer fitted with the dough hook, combine your flour, granulated sugar, brown sugar, and salt. Using a spatula or spoon, give this a toss until combined.

5. Swirl the brown butter around the bowl (this is to grease the sides of the bowl, which you'll use later) and pour the butter into the stand mixer. Add the milk/yeast mixture and the whole eggs plus the yolk, turn the mixer on low to combine for a minute, and then to medium to mix until the dough has formed. If the dough is really sticky and wet, add more flour, a tablespoon at a time, until the dough is one complete mixture. It's okay if it's a tad tacky, but it should all be combined. (You can also make the dough in a big bowl using a large spoon or a flat rubber spatula to combine.)

SWEETS & TREATS

BROWN BUTTER & MISO CINNAMON BABKA
continued

6. Add your babka dough to the buttered bowl, tossing to coat on all sides with the butter, and shape into a rough ball. Cover tightly and let sit until doubled in size, 2 to 3 hours at room temperature or 8 to 12 hours in the fridge. (If you keep your dough in the fridge overnight, the next day let it sit at room temperature, covered, for 2 to 3 hours, until warm to touch and easy to handle.)

7. **Make your Brown Butter & Miso Cinnamon Filling:** In a small saucepan, brown your butter using the same method as in step 2. While the butter is melting, use a little of it to brush all sides of two 9 by 5-inch loaf pans. Once the butter is browned, remove from the heat, and add your brown sugar, miso, cinnamon, and vanilla. Mix well until combined and cool for at least 15 minutes, stirring occasionally. As it sits it will firm up and turn into a thick, spreadable paste.

8. **Roll and bake:** Line the pans with a strip of parchment paper that hangs over the long sides so that the baked loaves are easier to remove. Punch down the dough with your fist. Flour a pastry slab or other work surface and transfer your dough to it. Divide into 2 equal portions. Roll out each portion on a floured surface into a 24 by 8-inch rectangle. Dividing the filling evenly, spread it along all sides and inside of each dough rectangle, leaving a 1/2-inch border on the sides of the dough.

9. Starting on a short side, tightly roll each piece of dough into a thick log. Pinch the ends together to seal. Transfer both logs to a large sheet pan and place in the freezer for 10 minutes to firm up.

10. Remove from the freezer and set on the work surface. With a serrated knife, trim about ½ inch off the ends of each log. Slice each log in half lengthwise and then form a braid by making an X in the middle with the two log halves, filling-side up. Fold over from the center on both sides, wrapping the log halves around each other as tight as you can, pinching at the ends to keep in place. Like an accordion, push both ends of the babka to shorten it up (so it fits in the pan) and transfer to a prepared loaf pan.

11. Cover tightly and let sit at room temperature until the dough rises slightly and fills out the pans, 2 to 3 hours.

12. Preheat your oven to 350°F.

13. Transfer to the oven and bake until your babkas turn a nice golden brown, without getting too dark, 35 to 45 minutes. To test doneness, you can use a thermometer; it should read 185° to 210°F.

14. Remove from the oven and brush simple syrup over your babkas. Let them cool in the pans for 5 minutes. Then transfer to a cutting board and let sit for 5 to 10 more minutes before slicing. Serve warm!

INDIVIDUAL MIXED-BERRY CRUMBLES

SERVES 4
1 HOUR

3 cups mixed fresh or frozen berries, such as blackberries, raspberries, and strawberries

2 tablespoons all-purpose flour, plus ½ cup

¼ cup granulated sugar, plus 2 tablespoons

Grated zest and juice of 1 medium lemon

4 tablespoons unsalted butter, cubed and cold

2 tablespoons packed light brown sugar

Pinch of kosher salt

Vanilla ice cream (optional), for serving

Ever since I can remember, my Aunt Lulu and Uncle Allan would make batches of berry crumble for the holidays. It's something they know I love and look forward to each year; naturally, a version of it deserves a special place in this book. This crumble is made with a base of strawberries, raspberries, and blackberries, and is served with a dollop of vanilla ice cream, which is the perfect complement to this warm dessert.

1. **Equipment:** Get out four 8-ounce ramekins or mini cocottes.

2. Preheat your oven to 350°F.

3. **Make your berry mixture:** In a medium bowl, combine the berries, 2 tablespoons of the all-purpose flour, ¼ cup of the granulated sugar, the lemon zest, and lemon juice. Toss to combine and set aside.

4. **Make your crumble topping:** In another medium bowl, combine the butter, brown sugar, kosher salt, and the remaining ½ cup flour and 2 tablespoons granulated sugar. Gently massage all these ingredients together until a fine, crumbly mixture is formed. (It might seem dry at first—that's okay. Just keep squeezing!)

5. Set the ramekins or cocottes on a baking sheet and divide your berry mixture among them. Top with the crumble topping.

6. Transfer to the oven and bake until the berries are juicy and bubbling, and the top of the crumble is a light brown hue, 45 to 50 minutes.

7. **To serve:** Remove from the oven and let cool for 5 minutes. Serve as is, or à la mode with a small scoop of vanilla ice cream (if using).

MAKES 6 PUFFS
1 HOUR

STRAWBERRY & CARDAMOM MASCARPONE PUFFS

1 (8-ounce) sheet frozen puff pastry

1 pound medium strawberries, hulled and quartered

2 tablespoons maple syrup

1 large egg, beaten, or whole milk, for brushing

8 ounces mascarpone

½ teaspoon ground cardamom

Pinch of kosher salt

Macerated strawberries are berries that sit in sugar (but here I'm using maple syrup) until their own juices are released and they become soft, tender, and syrupy. Add it in crispy puff pastry, with a cardamom mascarpone, and you have a simple yet impressive dessert. You can eat these puffs warm as they're ready, or you can prep everything ahead and serve when ready to eat!

1. Let your puff pastry thaw to room temperature, at least 30 minutes.

2. **Make your macerated strawberries:** In a medium bowl, toss the strawberries with 1 tablespoon of the maple syrup. Cover and refrigerate until serving, or up to overnight. The longer they sit, the more syrupy they will be.

3. Preheat your oven to 375°F. Line a large baking sheet with parchment paper.

4. Use a rolling pin to flatten out the puff pastry. Using a large round cookie cutter (3½ to 4 inches) or the large base of a medium cup, cut out 6 rounds and transfer to the baking sheet. Brush the tops of the pastry with egg wash or milk.

5. Transfer to the oven and bake until the top edges of the rounds are a light golden brown, 20 to 25 minutes. Remove it from the oven and let cool for a couple of minutes or until room temperature.

6. **Prepare the cardamom mascarpone:** While your puff pastry is baking, in a medium bowl, stir together the mascarpone, the remaining 1 tablespoon maple syrup, the cardamom, and salt. Refrigerate until serving.

7. Once cooled enough to handle, use your hands to split the pastry in the center to make two rounds.

8. **To serve:** Transfer the bottoms to a platter and spread your mascarpone over each round. Top with your macerated strawberries and finish with the top of the pastry to make a sandwich. You can eat it like a sandwich with your hands, or use a fork and knife.

LET'S DRINK SHALL WE?

MAKES ¾ CUP
5 MINUTES

SIMPLE SYRUP

1 cup granulated sugar

1 cup water

You can also make syrups with your favorite flavors, such as vanilla bean, rosemary, mint, cinnamon, and more! To infuse simple syrup, add the ingredient of your choice when you first heat your sugar and water. Strain out the ingredient, if necessary, and store.

Making simple syrup at home is easy and practically foolproof. It can be used in the Brown Butter & Miso Cinnamon Babka (page 241), as well as in the cocktails in this book. I often make simple syrup ahead of time and store it so it's always available for my coffee or matcha, too.

In a small saucepan, combine the sugar and water. Stir constantly over medium heat until the sugar has dissolved. Cool and store in an airtight container in the fridge for up to 1 month.

MAKES 1 COCKTAIL
15 MINUTES

APEROL MEZCAL MARGARITA WITH TAJÍN

Tajín seasoning, for rimming the glass

½ lemon, plus 1 ounce freshly squeezed lemon juice

Ice cubes

2 ounces mezcal

1 ounce Aperol

1 ounce Triple Sec

½ ounce freshly squeezed orange juice

Picture this: It's a sunny, summer day, you're sitting by the pool, and this tangy, smoky, and sweet tropical drink comes straight to your pool chair. Combining mezcal, a smoky, floral, and earthy spirit, with the sweetness of Aperol, an Italian aperitif, takes this cocktail to new heights, almost like an Aperol spritz meets a margarita.

1. Start by rimming your glass. Take a small plate and spread a thin layer of Tajín seasoning on it. Use the halved lemon to moisten a half-moon-shaped patch on the side of a glass. Dip the moistened part of the glass into the Tajín seasoning to coat it evenly. Set the glass aside.

2. In an ice-filled cocktail shaker, combine the mezcal, Aperol, Triple Sec, lemon juice, and orange juice and shake vigorously for 15 to 20 seconds. Fill your rimmed glass with fresh ice and strain your drink into the glass.

BLACKBERRY MAPLE BOURBON OLD-FASHIONED

MAKES 1 COCKTAIL
15 MINUTES

6 to 7 fresh blackberries, plus 1 or 2 for garnish

½ ounce maple syrup

4 to 5 dashes of orange bitters

1 ounce bourbon

Ice cubes

"You're getting the old-fashioned, right?" is something I will instantly ask Danny with a chuckle whenever we go out for drinks. He will always choose the classic drink, no matter what sort of variety or flavor profile it may be. This is a take on a classic old-fashioned, in honor of Danny's favorite pick. Muddled blackberries add a subtle earthiness, while the maple rounds it out by giving a sweet, almost caramel-like essence to pair alongside the smoky bourbon. It goes down easy and is a spirit-forward cocktail to serve alongside any meal, but might I suggest the Steak & Potatoes for Two with Asparagus & Bagna Cauda (page 189)?

1. In a mixing glass or a mason jar, combine the blackberries, maple syrup, and orange bitters. Muddle the blackberries with a muddler or the back of a spoon to release their flavors. Add the bourbon and ice. Stir with a large cocktail spoon vigorously for 15 to 20 seconds.

2. Strain the cocktail over a big ice cube in a rocks glass. Garnish with a couple of blackberries.

MAKES 1 COCKTAIL
15 MINUTES

LIME & BASIL GIN SOUR

8 to 10 large fresh basil leaves, plus sprigs for garnish

1 ounce Simple Syrup (page 250)

2 ounces gin

1 ounce fresh lime juice

1 egg white

Ice cubes

Tequila or vodka works, too!

Hands down, gin is my spirit of choice, while basil is one of my favorite herbs. Put them together and you have the perfect pairing. The herbaceous aroma from the muddled basil, shaken with fresh lime juice and gin, is the perfect symphony of ingredients. I love straining this into a chilled coupe glass, and the froth created from the egg white will look and taste like you just got it from a restaurant. A cocktail shaker is cool and all, but I find I get a really strong shake with a tightly sealed mason jar, without the hassle of trying to open the top of the icy cold shaker. If you know you know.

1. Place your glass of choice in the freezer for 5 to 10 minutes.

2. In a cocktail shaker or a mason jar, add your basil leaves and simple syrup. Gently muddle the basil leaves with a muddler or the back of a spoon to release their flavors.

3. Add the gin, lime juice, and egg white. Seal the container and dry shake vigorously for 15 to 20 seconds. This will help emulsify the egg white and create a frothy texture. Open the shaker and fill it with ice. Shake again for 15 to 20 seconds.

4. Strain the cocktail into your chilled glass, where the froth will form a layer on the top. Garnish with a sprig of fresh basil.

MAKES 1 COCKTAIL
15 MINUTES

MANGO, MANDARIN & GINGER SMOOTHIE WITH A TANGY SUMAC RIM

½ cup freshly squeezed mandarin or other orange juice (3 to 4 small oranges; one juiced half reserved)

Sumac, for rimming the glass

1 cup frozen mango chunks

1 or 2 thin slices peeled fresh ginger, peeled, roughly chopped

1 tablespoon honey

¼ cup well-chilled water or coconut water, plus more as needed

It should come as no surprise that I love sumac. It's citrusy, tangy, floral, and sweet, and works especially well as a rim for a mocktail or a smoothie. The citrusy notes from sumac work well with frozen mango, a splash of mandarin juice, and a slice of fresh ginger.

1. Run a spent mandarin half along the rim of a glass. Spread a thin layer of sumac on a small plate. Dip the rim of your glass into the sumac. Set the glass aside.

2. In a stand blender, combine your mandarin juice, mango, ginger, honey, and water. Blend until completely smooth. Adjust with more water as needed to reach your desired texture.

3. Pour carefully into your rimmed glass.

**MAKES 4 SMALL CUPS
(THIS IS A STRONG TEA!)
15 MINUTES**

GRANDPA'S PIPING HOT CHAI

6 green cardamom pods

1-inch piece unpeeled fresh ginger

10 black peppercorns

2 cups water

4 teaspoons loose black tea leaves or 2 black tea bags (my family uses PG Tips)

4 whole cloves

1 cinnamon stick

1 cup whole milk or nondairy milk

1 to 2 tablespoons granulated sugar

Originating in India, chai is a popular drink served throughout South Asia. It's made of brewed black tea (PG Tips is my family's favorite!), boiled with milk, sugar, and aromatics such as ginger, black peppercorns, cardamon, and cinnamon.

I was first introduced to chai when I was a little girl. I have fond memories of my grandparents, both born in India, driving up the street to the local Indian market every afternoon to pick up their piping hot chai. When my grandmother passed, my grandfather continued to go to the Indian market daily with his children and grandchildren. We would all anticipate our daily calls, usually around 3:30 p.m. "Where are you? I'm ready to go get my chai!" And every time he ordered he would holler the same thing: "I want it piping hot!" He continued to return to his favorite tea shop until he passed away in 2023. This chai's for my Grandpa Sas!

1. **Equipment:** Have a fine-mesh sieve ready.

2. With a heavy-bottomed pot on a cutting board, or in a mortar and pestle, lightly crush your cardamom, ginger, and black peppercorns to release their aromas. You don't need a powder here, just a quick crush, making sure the cardamom pods crack open.

3. In a small saucepan, combine the water, crushed spice mix, black tea, cloves, and cinnamon. Bring the mixture to a boil over high heat, stirring occasionally, and cook for 3 to 4 minutes.

4. Then add your milk and return to a boil for about 2 minutes. (Watch carefully to make sure it doesn't boil over!) You want to see a rolling boil, with bubbles and some foaming. Reduce the heat to medium-low and simmer for another 4 to 5 minutes.

5. While your chai is simmering, add the sugar to taste. Start with 1 tablespoon and adjust with more from there.

6. Strain the chai through the fine-mesh sieve into cups or mugs. Serve piping hot (just like my Grandpa Sas!).

All the Sauces, Dressings & Condiments Your Heart Desires

Sauces & Condiments

Creamy Avocado Ginger Salsa 133
–Auntie Nina's Spicy Slow-Braised Beef Chitanni 191
–Ancho Chile Shrimp Tacos with Creamy Avocado Ginger Salsa 133
–Fajita-Rubbed Chicken with Grilled Bell Peppers 166

Horseradish Cream 93
–Pecorino Paprika Polenta Fries 225
–Beet Soup with Fennel, Onions & Horseradish Cream 93

Mint Zhoug 201
–Shawarma-Spiced Whole Roasted Cauliflower with Garlicky Tahini & Quick-Pickled Onions 210
–Black Pepper & Coriander Rack of Lamb with Mint Zhoug & Chickpeas 201
–Spiced Lamb Meatballs with Feta, Tomato & Cucumber Salad 178

Minty-Lime Yogurt 89
–Turmeric Dal with Minty-Lime Yogurt & Crispy Onions 89
–Auntie Nina's Spicy Slow-Braised Beef Chitanni 191

Sambal Aioli 55
–Pecorino Paprika Polenta Fries 225
–Panzanella Toast with Sambal Aioli 55
–Skillet Hot Sauce & Brown Sugar Chicken Thighs with Frazzled Snap Peas 162

Spicy Miso Mayo 34
–Pecorino Paprika Polenta Fries 225
–Crispy Tempura Cauliflower Tossed in Spicy Miso Mayo 34

Sumac & Saffron Chili Crisp 32
–Spicy Crushed Cucumber Salad with Feta & Mint 72
–Turmeric Dal with Minty-Lime Yogurt & Crispy Onions 89
–Chili Crisp & Strawberry Baked Brie 42
–Spicy Peanut Noodles with Snap Peas & Scallions 119
–Seared Tuna Steaks with Ponzu, Crispy Garlic & Cucumbers 138
–Persian Shallot Dip with Sumac & Saffron Chili Crisp 32

Very Shallot-y Mayo 63
–MLT with Very Shallot-y Mayo 63
–Pecorino Paprika Polenta Fries 225

Zesty Crema 59
–Shakshuka Rancheros with Zesty Crema 59
–Fajita-Rubbed Chicken with Grilled Bell Peppers 166
–Ancho Chile Shrimp Tacos with Creamy Avocado Ginger Salsa 133

Dressings

Cilantro-Lime Vinaigrette 222

Gorgonzola Dressing 76
–Meyer Lemon & Harissa Wings 22

–Honey Buffalo Glazed Chicken with Shaved Carrots 169

Green Goddess Vinaigrette 79

Habanero Dressing 71

Orange Maple Poppy Seed Vinaigrette 83

Ranch-Ish Dressing 84
–Meyer Lemon & Harissa Wings 22
–Honey Buffalo Glazed Chicken with Shaved Carrots 169

Smashed Caper Dressing 68

Uncle Ira's "Good Dressing" 80

Crunchy Things

Bacon Bread Crumbs 76
–Anchovy Harissa Mussels & Linguine 128
–Steakhouse Wedge Salad with Gorgonzola Dressing & Bacon Bread Crumbs 76
–Charred Cabbage with Calabrian Chili Butter 209

Chili-Lime Strips 98

Pizza-ish Croutons 105

Sun-Dried Tomato & Vinegar Bread Crumbs 120
–Anchovy Harissa Mussels & Linguine 128
–Charred Cabbage with Calabrian Chili Butter 209
–Hazelnut Pesto Bucatini with Sun-Dried Tomato & Vinegar Bread Crumbs 120

Parties & Pairings

Al Fresco Nights

Meyer Lemon & Harissa Wings (page 22)

Steakhouse Wedge Salad with Gorgonzola Dressing & Bacon Bread Crumbs (page 76)

Beet & Peach Salad with Burrata, Toasted Hazelnuts & Green Goddess Vinaigrette (page 79)

Pomegranate Yogurt Marinated Grilled Chicken (page 174), Smash Burgers with Secret Sauce (page 186), or Coffee & Cayenne Rubbed Ribs with Mustard Barbecue Sauce (page 196)

Individual Mixed-Berry Crumbles (page 245) or Strawberry & Cardamom Mascarpone Puffs (page 246)

Lime & Basil Gin Sour (page 254) or Aperol Mezcal Margarita with Tajín (page 250)

Holiday Dinner

Curry & Honey Spiced Nuts (page 26)

Anchovy & Pepperoncini Olive Tapenade Crostini (page 60) or Chili Crisp & Strawberry Baked Brie (page 42)

Icy Crudités with Roasted Garlic Tarragon Yogurt Dip (page 28)

Radicchio & Fennel Salad with Orange Maple Poppy Seed Vinaigrette (page 83)

Really Good Roast Chicken (page 155)

Black Pepper & Coriander Rack of Lamb with Mint Zhoug & Chickpeas (page 201)

Lemony Couscous with a Kick (page 229)

Za'atar-Roasted Kabocha Squash with Pomegranate Dressing (page 226)

Brown Butter & Miso Cinnamon Babka (page 241) or Tahini Chocolate Chip Cookies with Toasted Sesame Seeds (page 232)

Blackberry Maple Bourbon Old-Fashioned (page 253)

A Weeknight Meal That's Not Boring

Steakhouse Wedge Salad with Gorgonzola Dressing & Bacon Bread Crumbs (page 76)

Garlic & Old Bay Brick Chicken with Schmaltzy Baby Potatoes (page 170)

Brown Sugar Hojicha Banana Bread (page 235)

Impressing Your New Persian Partner

Persian Shallot Dip with Sumac & Saffron Chili Crisp (page 32)

Kashke Bademjan with a Lotta Kashk (page 56)

Spicy Crushed Cucumber Salad with Feta & Mint (page 72)

Grilled Sumac Shell-On Shrimp (page 150)

Onion Butter Kebab Koobideh with Radishes & Herbs (page 182)

A Pot o' Rice (page 228)

Mango, Mandarin & Ginger Smoothie with a Tangy Sumac Rim (page 257)

Pasta & Pizza

Scallop & Radish Crudo with Chile & Citrus (page 37)

Little Gem Caesar Salad with Habanero Dressing & Sourdough Bread Crumbs (page 71)

Danny's Sicilian Pizza with Garlicky Oil (page 46)

Lamb Bolognese with Fennel & Ricotta (page 115)

Maple Chili Glazed Carrots with Carrot-Top Salsa Verde (page 206)

Salted Caramel Chocolate Mousse (page 239)

My Family Dinner

Butter Lettuce & Avocado Salad with Uncle Ira's "Good Dressing" (page 80)

Turmeric Dal with Minty-Lime Yogurt & Crispy Onions (page 89)

Auntie Nina's Spicy Slow-Braised Beef Chitanni (page 191)

Creamy Avocado Ginger Salsa (page 133)

Roasted Broccolini with Cilantro-Lime Vinaigrette (page 222)

A Pot o' Rice (page 228)

Date Night in for Two

Scallop & Radish Crudo with Chile & Citrus (page 37)

Endive & Whole-Grain Mustard Salad (page 75)

Steak & Potatoes for Two with Asparagus & Bagna Cauda (page 189)

Blackberry Maple Bourbon Old-Fashioned (page 253)

Snack & Sip

Curry & Honey Spiced Nuts (page 26)

Icy Crudités with Roasted Garlic Tarragon Yogurt Dip (page 28)

Ponzu & Togarashi–Marinated Olives (page 38)

Chili Crisp & Strawberry Baked Brie (page 42)

Anchovy & Pepperoncini Olive Tapenade Crostini (page 60)

Tahini Chocolate Chip Cookies with Toasted Sesame Seeds (page 232)

Blackberry Maple Bourbon Old-Fashioned (page 253)

Lime & Basil Gin Sour (page 254)

Acknowledgments

To my husband, Danny, this book is not mine alone; it is shared with the best partner anyone could ask for. Thank you for trying every recipe in this book, for your honest feedback, and for always pushing me to be the best version of myself. Thank you for being my constant support, and for loving me.

To my mom, Marlene, who has always taught me to follow my intuition, pursue my passions, and live with purpose. Thank you for spending countless days with me helping craft the headnotes. This book wouldn't be what it is without your input and endless guidance.

To my dad, Oren, thank you for being my number one fan and encouraging and supporting my dreams. I know that if a recipe has your stamp of approval, it's always good to go.

To my sister, Alexa, who selflessly sacrificed so much of her time to help me through this process. I am deeply grateful for you and the incredible bond we share—not just as sisters but as best friends.

To my brother, Jake, thank you for always being there for me at a moment's notice and never hesitating when I need anything.

To my Aunt Lulu, Uncle Allan, Aunt Nina, Uncle Ira, Aunt Renee, Uncle Norman, Aunt Florette, Uncle Ruven, and all my special cousins and family members, this book is a love letter to our family. Thank you for always opening your hearts and your homes.

To Jessica and Jay, thank you for introducing me to new foods, making sure dessert was always served after dinner, and showing me how food is the secret ingredient that adds to amazing memories.

To my grandparents, whose legacy has left an indelible mark on my heart. Because of you I understand that food is not just about nourishment; it's about family, home, and memories.

To the amazing recipe testers, Ali Slagle and Caroline Lange, this book wouldn't be what it is without your invaluable feedback and tireless testing. **Ali,** thank you for pushing me out of my comfort zone and always teaching me something new. **Caroline,** your attention to detail made the recipes in this book extraordinary.

To the **Lindsey Eats Team:** CAA, **Rachel O'Brien** for your light and positive energy, and for always supporting me as my agent and friend. To my book agent, **Anthony Mattero,** you've been instrumental in helping me refine my style, define my theme, and shape this book into what it is today, starting from the very beginning of our proposal together. **Arielle Harris,** thank you for your belief in me. I'm grateful for your dedication in this project.

To the Ten Speed team: To my editor, **Kelly Snowden,** thank you for believing in me since day one. Your trust has given me the confidence to pour my heart into this book. Thank you for giving me this opportunity to fulfill a dream I've had since I was a little girl. To the creative director **Emma Campion,** your talent is unmatched, thank you for crafting and refining my vision. I've learned so much from you. **To Annie Marino,** for bringing the vision of the typography to life from day one.

To the photography dream team: It's been a joy to collaborate with such talented, passionate creators. **To my photographer, Eva Kolenko,** you turned these images into something beyond what I could have ever imagined. **Emily Caneer,** you are a food styling wizard, thank you for meticulously making everything look effortless. Thank you, **Carrie Beyer,** for your help and positive energy. **Genesis Vallejo,** you went the extra mile with the props, colors, and textures throughout the book.

To **Debs Lim,** the beyond-talented illustrator. Your illustrations brought the color palette, typography, and recipes to life.

To my audience and readers, this journey would not have been possible without you. Every one of you reading these words has played a part in making this a reality. There isn't a day that goes by that I'm not deeply grateful for this incredible community—your messages, your comments, and the way you've brought my recipes to your tables, sharing them with friends and family.

Index

Note: Page references in *italics* indicate photographs.

A

Anchovy
    Harissa Mussels & Linguine, 128, *129*
    & Pepperoncini Olive Tapenade Crostini, 60, *61*
Aperol Mezcal Margarita with Tajín, 250, *251*
Asparagus and Bagna Cauda, Steak & Potatoes for Two with, 188, *189*–90
Avocado
    & Butter Lettuce Salad with Uncle Ira's "Good Dressing," 80, *81*
    Ginger Salsa, Creamy, Ancho Chile Shrimp Tacos with, *132*, 133

B

Banana Bread, Brown Sugar Hojicha, *234*, 235
Beans
    Black Pepper & Coriander Rack of Lamb with Mint Zhoug & Chickpeas, 201–2, *203*
    Butter, & Smashed Olives, Aleppo-Braised Chicken Legs with, *164*, 165
    Kinda Niçoise with Farro & Smashed Caper Dressing, 68, *69*
    Rosemary Butter, with Heavy Pepper & Pecorino, 64, *65*
    White, & Dill Chimichurri, Seared Scallops with, *144*, 145
    White Miso & Scallion Brothy, *100*, 101
Beef
    Chitanni, Auntie Nina's Spicy Slow-Braised, 191–92, *193*
    Chitanni, Provolone & Shishito Cheesesteak, *194*, 195
    Galbi-Inspired Steak with Quick Pear Kimchi, *198*, 199–200
    Onion Butter Kebab Koobideh with Radishes & Herbs, 182–85, *183*
    Smash Burgers with Secret Sauce, 186, *187*
    Steak & Potatoes for Two with Asparagus and Bagna Cauda, 188, *189*–90
Beet
    & Peach Salad with Burrata, Toasted Hazelnuts & Green Goddess Vinaigrette, 78, *79*
    Soup with Fennel, Onions & Horseradish Cream, *92*, 93
Berry, Mixed-, Crumbles, Individual, *244*, 245
Blackberry Maple Bourbon Old-Fashioned, *252*, 253
Bourbon Old-Fashioned, Blackberry Maple, *252*, 253
Branzino, Grilled Whole, with Herbs & Loads of Lime, *136*, 137
Bread. *See also* Toasts
    Banana, Brown Sugar Hojicha, *234*, 235
    Brown Butter & Miso Cinnamon Babka, 241–42, *243*
Broccolini
    Roasted, with Cilantro-Lime Vinaigrette, *222*, 223
    & Smoked Gouda Soup, Cream of, 90, *91*
Brussels Sprouts, Chili Garlic, with Furikake, 218, *219*
Burgers, Smash, with Secret Sauce, 186, *187*

C

Cabbage
    Charred, with Calabrian Chili Butter, *208*, 209
    & Leek, Caramelized, Pasta, *126*, 127
    Napa, Stovetop Miso Halibut en Papillote with, *142*, 143
Calabrian Chili
    Butter, Charred Cabbage with, *208*, 209
    Tomato Soup with Pizza-ish Croutons, *104*, 105
Cantaloupe, Cucumber & Tomato Salad with Ranch-ish Dressing, 84, *85*
Carrots
    Maple Chili Glazed, with Carrot-Top Salsa Verde, 206, *207*
    Shaved, Honey Buffalo Glazed Chicken with, *168*, 169
Cauliflower
    Crispy Tempura, Tossed in Spicy Miso Mayo, 34, *35*
    Shawarma-Spiced Whole Roasted, with Garlicky Tahini & Quick-Pickled Onions, 210–12, *211*
Chai, Grandpa's Piping Hot, 258, *259*
Cheese
    Beet & Peach Salad with Burrata, Toasted Hazelnuts & Green Goddess Vinaigrette, 78, *79*
    Chili Crisp & Strawberry Baked Brie, 42, *43*
    Chitanni, Provolone & Shishito Cheesesteak, *194*, 195
    Cream of Broccolini & Smoked Gouda Soup, 90, *91*
    Danny's Sicilian Pizza with Garlicky Oil, 46–49, *47*
    One-Pot French Onion & Shallot Soup with Sourdough Toasts, 102, *103*
    Pan-Fried Panko-Crusted Eggplant with Jammy Cherry Tomatoes & Burrata, 213–14, *215*

Pecorino Paprika Polenta Fries, *224*, *225*
Spicy Crushed Cucumber Salad with Feta & Mint, *72*, *73*
Steakhouse Wedge Salad with Gorgonzola Dressing & Bacon Bread Crumbs, *76*, *77*

Chicken
   & Celery Salad, Curried, Sandwiches, *160*, *161*
   Fajita-Rubbed, with Grilled Bell Peppers, *166*, *167*
   Garlic & Old Bay Brick, with Schmaltzy Baby Potatoes, *170*, *171*
   Honey Buffalo Glazed, with Shaved Carrots, *168*, *169*
   Legs, Aleppo-Braised, with Butter Beans & Smashed Olives, *164*, *165*
   Meyer Lemon & Harissa Wings, *22*, *23*
   Piccata, Orangey, with Jammy Shallots, 157–58, *159*
   Pomegranate Yogurt Marinated Grilled, *174*, *175*
   Rice, & Tomato Soup, Grandma Daisy's, 94–97, *95*
   Roast, Really Good, *154*, 155–56
   Schnitzel, Crispy Sesame & Herb, *172*, *173*
   Thighs, Skillet Hot Sauce & Brown Sugar, with Frazzled Snap Peas, *162*, *163*

Chocolate
   Chip Tahini Cookies with Toasted Sesame Seeds, *232*, *233*
   Mousse, Salted Caramel, *238*, *239*–40

Cookies, Tahini Chocolate Chip, with Toasted Sesame Seeds, *232*, *233*

Couscous
   Lemony, with a Kick, 229
   & Zucchini Tzatziki, Crispy-Skinned Salmon with, *148*, 149

Cucumber(s)
   Cantaloupe, & Tomato Salad with Ranch-ish Dressing, *84*, *85*
   Feta, and Tomato Salad, Spiced Lamb Meatballs with, *178*, *179*
   Kinda Niçoise with Farro & Smashed Caper Dressing, *68*, *69*
   Panzanella Toast with Sambal Aioli, *54*, 55
   Spicy Crushed, Salad with Feta & Mint, *72*, *73*

D
Dal, Turmeric, with Minty-Lime Yogurt & Crispy Onions, *88*, 89

Dips
   Caramelized Five-Allium, Topped with Salmon Roe, *29*, *30*
   Kashke Bademjan with a Lotta Kashk, *56*, *57*
   Persian Shallot, with Sumac & Saffron Chili Crisp, *31*, 32–33
   Roasted Garlic Tarragon Yogurt, Icy Crudités with, 28

Drinks, list of, 7

E
Eggplant
   Kashke Bademjan with a Lotta Kashk, *56*, *57*
   Pan-Fried Panko-Crusted, with Jammy Cherry Tomatoes & Burrata, 213–14, *215*

Eggs
   Kinda Niçoise with Farro & Smashed Caper Dressing, *68*, *69*
   Shakshuka Rancheros with Zesty Crema, *58*, *59*

Endive & Whole-Grain Mustard Salad, *74*, *75*

F
Farro & Smashed Caper Dressing, Kinda Niçoise with, *68*, *69*
Fennel & Radicchio Salad with Orange Maple Poppy Seed Vinaigrette, *82*, *83*

G
Garlic
   & Old Bay Brick Chicken with Schmaltzy Baby Potatoes, *170*, *171*
   Roasted, Tarragon Yogurt Dip, Icy Crudités with, 28

Gin Sour, Lime & Basil, *254*, *255*
Gochujang Soju Rigatoni, *122*, *123*
Grapefruit & Ginger Cured Salmon on Bagels, *146*, *147*

H
Halibut en Papillote, Stovetop Miso, with Napa Cabbage, *142*, *143*
Hazelnut Pesto Bucatini with Sun-Dried Tomato & Vinegar Bread Crumbs, *120*, *121*

L
Lamb
   Black Pepper & Coriander Rack of, with Mint Zhoug & Chickpeas, 201–2, *203*
   Bolognese with Fennel & Ricotta, *114*, 115–16
   Meatballs, Spiced, with Feta, Tomato & Cucumber Salad, *178*, *179*

Leek
    & Baked Potato Soup, Loaded, with Paprika Butter, 106, *107*
    & Cabbage, Caramelized, Pasta, 126, *127*
Lentils. *See* Dal
Lettuce
    Butter, & Avocado Salad with Uncle Ira's "Good Dressing," 80, *81*
    Little Gem Caesar Salad with Habanero Dressing & Sourdough Bread Crumbs, 70, *71*
    Steakhouse Wedge Salad with Gorgonzola Dressing & Bacon Bread Crumbs, 76, *77*
Lime & Basil Gin Sour, 254, *255*

M

Mandarin, Mango & Ginger Smoothie with a Tangy Sumac Rim, 256, *257*
Mango, Mandarin & Ginger Smoothie with a Tangy Sumac Rim, 256, *257*
Meatballs, Spiced Lamb, with Feta, Tomato & Cucumber Salad, 178, *179*
Mezcal Aperol Margarita with Tajín, 250, *251*
Mousse, Salted Caramel Chocolate, 238, *239*–40
Mushroom
    "Escargots" with Parsley Butter, 44, *45*
    Miso Mascarpone Pappardelle, 124, *125*
Mussels, Anchovy Harissa, & Linguine, 128, *129*

N

Noodles, Spicy Peanut, with Snap Peas & Scallions, 118, *119*
Nuts. *See also specific nuts*
    Curry & Honey Spiced, 26, *27*

O

Olive(s)
    Ponzu & Togarashi–Marinated, 38, *39*
    Smashed, & Butter Beans, Aleppo-Braised Chicken Legs with, 164, *165*
    Tapenade, Anchovy & Pepperoncini, Crostini, 60, *61*
Onion(s)
    Caramelized Five-Allium Dip Topped with Salmon Roe, 29, *30*
    Caramelized, & Sour Cream Potatoes, 220, *221*
    Quick-Pickled, & Garlicky Tahini, Shawarma-Spiced Whole Roasted Cauliflower with, 210–12, *211*
    & Shallot Soup, One-Pot French, with Sourdough Toasts, 102, *103*

P

Pasta
    Anchovy Harissa Mussels & Linguine, 128, *129*
    Buttery Saffron & Sungold Tomato, 110, *111*
    Caramelized Leek & Cabbage, 126, *127*
    Hazelnut Pesto Bucatini with Sun-Dried Tomato & Vinegar Bread Crumbs, 120, *121*
    Lamb Bolognese with Fennel & Ricotta, 114, *115*–16
    Minty, with Hot Italian Sausage & Red Chard, 112, *113*
    Mushroom Miso Mascarpone Pappardelle, 124, *125*
    Soju Gochujang Rigatoni, 122, *123*
Peach & Beet Salad with Burrata, Toasted Hazelnuts & Green Goddess Vinaigrette, 78, *79*
Peanut Noodles, Spicy, with Snap Peas & Scallions, 118, *119*
Pears, Red Wine–Poached, with Vanilla Yogurt & Pistachios, 236, *237*
Peas, Snap
    Frazzled, Skillet Hot Sauce & Brown Sugar Chicken Thighs with, 162, *163*
    & Scallions, Spicy Peanut Noodles with, 118, *119*
Peppers
    Chitanni, Provolone & Shishito Cheesesteak, 194, *195*
    Grilled Bell, Fajita-Rubbed Chicken with, 166, *167*
Pizza, Danny's Sicilian, with Garlicky Oil, 46–49, *47*
Polenta Fries, Pecorino Paprika, 224, *225*
Pomegranate
    Dressing, Za'atar-Roasted Kabocha Squash with, 226, *227*
    Yogurt Marinated Grilled Chicken, 174, *175*
Pork
    Coffee & Cayenne Rubbed Ribs with Mustard Barbecue Sauce, 196, *197*
    Minty Pasta with Hot Italian Sausage & Red Chard, 112, *113*
    MLT with Very Shallot-y Mayo, 62, *63*
Potato(es)
    & Leek Soup, Loaded, Baked, with Paprika Butter, 106, *107*
    Schmaltzy Baby, Garlic & Old Bay Brick Chicken with, 170, *171*
    Sour Cream & Caramelized Onion, 220, *221*
    & Steak for Two with Asparagus and Bagna Cauda, 188, *189*–90

R

Radicchio & Fennel Salad with Orange Maple Poppy Seed Vinaigrette, 82, *83*
Radish(es)
    & Herbs, Onion Butter Kebab Koobideh with, 182–85, *183*
    & Scallop Crudo with Chile & Citrus, 36, *37*
    Sheet Pan Salt & Pepper, 216, *217*

Recipes
    ingredients, 14
    notes on, 12–13
    pairing with sauces, dressings
        & condiments, 261
    parties & pairings, 263–64
    tools and tips, 17–18
Rice
    Chicken, & Tomato Soup,
        Grandma Daisy's, 94–97, *95*
    A Pot o', 228

S

Salads, list of, 5
Salmon
    Crispy-Skinned, with Couscous
        & Zucchini Tzatziki, *148*, 149
    Grapefruit & Ginger Cured, on
        Bagels, 146, *147*
Sandwiches
    Chitanni, Provolone & Shishito
        Cheesesteak, *194*, 195
    Curried Chicken & Celery Salad,
        160, 161
    MLT with Very Shallot-y Mayo,
        62, 63
Scallop(s)
    & Radish Crudo with Chile &
        Citrus, *36*, 37
    Seared, with Dill Chimichurri &
        White Beans, *144*, 145
Shallot Dip, Persian, with Sumac &
    Saffron Chili Crisp, *31*, 32–33
Shrimp
    Ancho Chile Tacos with Creamy
        Avocado Ginger Salsa,
        132, 133
    Grilled Sumac Shell-On,
        150, *151*
Simple Syrup, 250
Smoothie, Mango, Mandarin &
    Ginger, with a Tangy Sumac
    Rim, *256*, 257
Snacks & apps, list of, 5
Soju Gochujang Rigatoni, *122*, 123
Soups, list of, 5
Squash, Kabocha, Za'atar-
    Roasted, with Pomegranate
    Dressing, 226, *227*
Steelhead Trout, Gochujang
    Slow-Roasted, with Cherry
    Tomatoes, 134, *135*
Strawberry
    & Cardamom Mascarpone
        Puffs, 246, *247*
    & Chili Crisp Baked Brie, 42, *43*
Sweets & treats, list of, 7
Syrup, Simple, 250

T

Tacos, Ancho Chile Shrimp, with
    Creamy Avocado Ginger Salsa,
    132, 133
Tahini Chocolate Chip Cookies
    with Toasted Sesame Seeds,
    232, *233*
Toasts
    Anchovy & Pepperoncini Olive
        Tapenade Crostini, 60, *61*
    Panzanella, with Sambal Aioli,
        54, 55
    Sourdough, One-Pot French
        Onion & Shallot Soup with,
        102, *103*
Tomato(es)
    Cherry, Gochujang Slow-
        Roasted Steelhead Trout
        with, 134, *135*
    & Chicken Rice Soup, Grandma
        Daisy's, 94–97, *95*
    Creamy Tortilla Soup with
        Chili-Lime Strips, 98, *99*
    Cucumber, & Cantaloupe Salad
        with Ranch-ish Dressing,
        84, *85*
    Danny's Sicilian Pizza with
        Garlicky Oil, 46–49, *47*
    Feta, & Cucumber Salad,
        Spiced Lamb Meatballs
        with, 178, *179*
    Jammy Cherry, & Burrata,
        Pan-Fried Panko-Crusted
        Eggplant with, 213–14, *215*
    Panzanella Toast with Sambal
        Aioli, *54*, 55
    Shakshuka Rancheros with
        Zesty Crema, *58*, 59
    Soup, Calabrian Chili, with
        Pizza-ish Croutons, *104*, 105
    Sungold, & Saffron Pasta,
        Buttery, *110*, 111
Tortilla(s)
    Ahi Tuna Aguachile Verde with
        Tostadas, *24*, 25
    Ancho Chile Shrimp Tacos with
        Creamy Avocado Ginger
        Salsa, *132*, 133
    Shakshuka Rancheros with
        Zesty Crema, *58*, 59
    Soup, Creamy, with Chili-Lime
        Strips, 98, *99*
Tuna
    Ahi, Aguachile Verde with
        Tostadas, *24*, 25
    Steaks, Seared, with Ponzu,
        Crispy Garlic & Cucumbers,
        138, *139*

V

Vegetables. *See also specific
    vegetables*
    Icy Crudités with Roasted
        Garlic Tarragon Yogurt
        Dip, 28

W

Walnut Brown Butter Vinaigrette,
    Flaky Whitefish with, *140*, 141
Whitefish, Flaky, with Brown
    Butter Walnut Vinaigrette,
    140, 141

Y

Yogurt
    Marinated Labneh Balls with
        Harissa & Aleppo Pepper,
        52, *53*
    Persian Shallot Dip with Sumac
        & Saffron Chili Crisp, *31*,
        32–33
    Roasted Garlic Tarragon Dip,
        Icy Crudités with, 28

Some of the recipes in this book include undercooked eggs, meat, or fish. When these foods are consumed undercooked, there is always the risk that bacteria, which is killed by proper cooking, may be present. Because of the health risks associated with the consumption of bacteria that can be present in undercooked eggs, meat, and fish, these foods should not be consumed by infants, small children, pregnant women, the elderly, or any persons who may be immunocompromised.

Ten Speed Press
An imprint of the Crown Publishing Group
A division of Penguin Random House LLC
1745 Broadway
New York, NY 10019
tenspeed.com
penguinrandomhouse.com

Text copyright © 2025 by Lindsey Baruch
Photographs copyright © 2025 by Eva Kolenko
Illustrations copyright © 2025 by Debs Lim
Penguin Random House values and supports copyright. Copyright fuels creativity, encourages diverse voices, promotes free speech, and creates a vibrant culture. Thank you for buying an authorized edition of this book and for complying with copyright laws by not reproducing, scanning, or distributing any part of it in any form without permission. You are supporting writers and allowing Penguin Random House to continue to publish books for every reader. Please note that no part of this book may be used or reproduced in any manner for the purpose of training artificial intelligence technologies or systems.

TEN SPEED PRESS and the Ten Speed Press colophon are registered trademarks of Penguin Random House LLC.

Typefaces: Fontfabric's Mueller and The League of Moveable Type's League Spartan

Library of Congress Cataloging-in-Publication Data
Names: Baruch, Lindsey, author. | Kolenko, Eva, photographer. Title: Something delicious : 100 recipes for everyday cooking / by Lindsey Baruch of Lindsey Eats ; photography by Eva Kolenko. Identifiers: LCCN 2024042907 (print) | LCCN 2024042908 (ebook) | ISBN 9780593835456 (hardcover) | ISBN 9780593835463 (ebook) Subjects: LCSH: Cooking. | LCGFT: Cookbooks.

Classification: LCC TX714 .B37238 2025 (print) | LCC TX714 (ebook) | DDC 641.5—dc23/eng/20241029
LC record available at https://lccn.loc.gov/2024042907
LC ebook record available at https://lccn.loc.gov/2024042908

Hardcover ISBN 978-0-593-83545-6
Ebook ISBN 978-0-593-83546-3

Acquiring editor: Kelly Snowden
Editorial assistant: Gabby Ureña Matos
Art director & designer: Emma Campion
Chapter-opener typographer: Annie Marino
Production designers: Mari Gill and Faith Hague
Production editor: Natalie Blachere
Production: Philip Leung
Food stylist: Emily Caneer
Food stylist assistant: Carrie Beyer
Location food stylist assistant: Hristina Misafiris
Prop stylist: Genesis Vallejo
Location photo assistant: Louis Heredia
Photo retoucher: Eva Kolenko
Copy editor: Kate Slate
Proofreaders: Patricia Dailey and Miriam Garron
Indexer: Elizabeth Parson
Publicist: Natalie Yera-Campbell
Marketer: Chloe Aryeh

Manufactured in China

10 9 8 7 6 5 4 3 2 1

First Edition

The authorized representative in the EU for product safety and compliance is Penguin Random House Ireland, Morrison Chambers, 32 Nassau Street, Dublin D02 YH68, Ireland, https://eu-contact.penguin.ie.

"I'm beyond thrilled to have Lindsey's debut cookbook, *Something Delicious*, on my kitchen shelves. It's a must-have for anyone looking to turn their kitchen into a sanctuary for simple, stunning meals and effortless hosting. This book is packed with creativity and bold flavors to keep every food lover inspired!"

—**Alex Snodgrass**, *New York Times* bestselling author and creator of The Defined Dish

"I can honestly say this is the *most* appropriately titled book because when I'm looking for something delicious, Lindsey is one of the first people I go to. This book strings effortlessly between her LA-fresh perspective, Persian influence, and comfort cooking. The fish chapter is already calling my name."

—**Justine Doiron**, *New York Times* bestselling author of *Justine Cooks*

"As two gals who live and breathe modern home cooking, we are absolutely thrilled about Lindsey's new cookbook. This collection of recipes feels both adventurous and completely doable. This is the kind of cookbook that will have you racing to the kitchen, eager to try everything. Trust us, you need this book in your life!"

—**Holly Erickson** and **Natalie Mortimer**, creators of The Modern Proper

"If there's one thing I can say about Lindsey, it's that her recipes never miss! Every single page of her beautiful cookbook showcases her passion and creativity for delicious food—you are going to want to make every single dish!"

—**Chris Joe**, creator of CJ Eats

"Lindsey's debut cookbook, *Something Delicious*, is a special extension of Lindsey's culinary approach, and everyone in your life needs a copy STAT! You can tell that each recipe has been carefully tested, thought out, and created to not only bring delicious, elevated meals to the table but to empower people to have fun—and success—in the kitchen, every single time."

—**Nicole Keshishian Modic**, founder of @kalejunkie and author of *Love to Eat*

"Lindsey's undeniable flair, brightness, and unique cooking style translate beautifully through her photos and recipes. This cookbook showcases so many flavor combinations, preparations, and fun foods. I can't wait to feed my friends and family these delicious recipes."

—**Nicole Enayati**, culinary producer and podcast host

"In a mouthwateringly vibrant and flavor-packed debut, Lindsey does what millions know her to do best: Make you drool at recipes that you *actually* want to cook and eat. With each story and dish, Lindsey packs the book with panache and recipes that will make you return again and again."

—**Eitan Bernath**, chef, author, and principal culinary contributor of *The Drew Barrymore Show*